A DIFFERENT
WAY TO WIN

DAN ROONEY'S STORY
FROM THE SUPER BOWL TO THE ROONEY RULE

JIM ROONEY

By Jim Rooney

With Contributions From:
Judy Battista
Terry Golway
Jeremi Duru

Additional Support:
Kelsey Morris
Jill Berardi
Brittany Shaffer
Bob Labriola
Mike Prisuta
John Allison
Stephanie Rooney

Special Thanks to:
Patricia Rooney
Art Rooney II
Roger Goodell

ISBN: 978-1-7334049-1-4 (Paperback Edition)
ISBN: 978-1-7334049-0-7 (Hardcover Edition)
ISBN: 978-1-7334049-2-1 (ebook Edition)

Cover photography by Pittsburgh Steelers (Mike Fabus)
Cover and Book design by Nium
Foreword by Joe Greene

Visit www.adifferentwaytowin.com

DEDICATED TO:

KATHLEEN, RITA AND JOAN

TABLE OF CONTENTS

FOREWORD

BY JOE GREENE

IT'S BEEN A LONG TIME, BUT I STILL REMEMBER THE DAY I MET DAN ROONEY. The Steelers had drafted me out of North Texas State in the first round in 1969, but I hadn't signed yet. I came up to Pittsburgh with my agent and met Mr. Rooney, as I called him then, in the Steelers' offices in the Roosevelt Hotel in the city's downtown. We talked a bit, and he asked me what I was doing. I told him I had been working out, which actually wasn't true. I had been holding out since the draft, and I wasn't exactly in shape. I don't think I fooled him.

After we figured out my contract and Mr. Rooney's father, Art, gave me a cigar —which I still have—I drove to training camp with Dan, whom I now refer to as "the Ambassador" in honor of his time as the U.S. envoy to Ireland as well as his role as a great representative of the NFL and of his home, Pittsburgh. I was pretty quiet during the trip, but the Ambassador filled the silence by telling me how much I would love Pittsburgh, although, knowing I was from Texas, he did mention that it occasionally got cold in western Pennsylvania.

I remember thinking how young he was at the time, and that he seemed genuinely interested in talking to me. Believe me, on that summer afternoon in 1969, I could not have imagined that one day Dan Rooney would ask me to present him when he was inducted into the Pro Football Hall of Fame in Canton, Ohio.

In fact, that seemed even more unlikely during my rookie season. I was a pretty bad actor on the field. I got thrown out of a few games, got into fights, and once against the Eagles, I grabbed a game ball before Philadelphia could snap it, heaved it into the stands, and stormed off the field. I was being held and the officials weren't calling it, so I was pretty mad. The officials were shocked.

Flash forward 13 years: I'm back in his office, telling him that I want to retire after so many great seasons with the Steelers. And he sits back and says, "Joe, remember that game in your rookie year when you threw the ball into the stands?" And I thought, "Oh, my goodness. Thirteen years have gone by and he never said a word about this." And then he said, "Joe, I felt the same way you did."

Another time, I remember treating a newspaper reporter very poorly. When the Ambassador found out about the incident he didn't scold me or go into a tirade. He clearly and effectively said, "Joe that is not how we do things around here." I thought that on any other team, they might have cut me or traded me after that first season. But Dan Rooney let me grow into a man. He saw that I was highly emotional and did some immature things. But he allowed me to find myself. Just a few years later, I was named captain of the Steelers, and at the time, I was anything but a captain. But that changed my attitude, and my bad acting just went away. I got the feeling that the Ambassador anticipated how I would react, that he saw something in me that I didn't know about myself.

That was the Dan Rooney I came to know. He was authentic, he had values, he knew how to play the long game when others were looking for short-term gain, and he believed in doing the right thing.

He used a phrase that I've never forgotten: "Let it soak." It was something I heard often when I was that young, emotional player. He'd simply tell me, "Let it soak." Think about it. Sleep on it. Consider the implications of your actions. That's what he meant.

He also was no pushover. Yes, he was quiet, but that was part of his inner strength. After my rookie year, I thought I deserved a raise because despite all the bad stuff, I had a pretty good season. So I went into the office and said, "Mr. Rooney, I think I need a raise." And he said, "Joe, I'm not going to give you one quarter." And the way he said it—well, I can't describe it, but I just started laughing. And the negotiation was over.

And years later, I interviewed for the head coaching job that Bill Cowher eventually got. The Ambassador summoned me to his office and said, "Joe, we're not going to hire you as head coach." I don't deny it—I was disappointed at first. But by the time I left the building, I was relieved because I realized he was right. It was the first time in my life and maybe the only time that I got "no" for an answer and felt comfortable with it. If Dan Rooney said I wasn't ready, then I wasn't ready. I trusted him.

I saw another side of the Ambassador while I was working as a scout for the Steelers. This was the business side of the man who took a team that had been always on the wrong end of the standings and turned it into a dynasty. He spoke with other front-office people in a quiet and matter-of-fact way, often explaining how he wanted things done—the right way.

During those years, I saw how impactful he was as a leader, not only as the owner of a team but as a leader of the National Football League. The other owners really listened to him, and that's because he had a reputation for being insightful, factual and honest. Looking back to even before I became a Steeler, I think his attitude, particularly his ability to see the big picture, was really important. When the old AFL joined the NFL to create the league we know today, he and his father put self-interest aside by agreeing to join the new American Football Conference. That was a key moment in the merger, and we all know what happened after that.

He also played an important role in another key moment, this one far from his hometown of Pittsburgh. During his stint as U.S. ambassador to Ireland, appointed by President Barack Obama, I have been told by many that he applied the same principles that guided his stewardship of the Steelers. My reaction was always: I would not expect anything else. He had long been an advocate for peace in Ireland, and as ambassador, he used his influence to help the healing process and bring prosperity to the land of his ancestors.

When you consider the man's character, values, acumen and his profound sense of fairness, it makes sense that Dan Rooney was the person who pushed for a hiring policy that now bears his name—the Rooney Rule. He saw an injustice—the league's coaches were almost all white in a league where most players are African-American. He persuaded the other owners to adopt a policy requiring management to interview minority candidates for head coaching vacancies beginning in 2003. That policy has been extended to other management vacancies in the years since.

The Rooney Rule is something the NFL desperately needs. It gives minorities an opportunity, at a minimum, to get into the pipeline for coaching and other jobs. It also gives minorities a chance to experience the job interview process, to learn what kinds of questions are asked, and to figure out how to prepare for an interview. If you're not getting interviews, you don't know how to answer those questions, and you're not getting into the pipeline. So the Rooney Rule strengthens the entire league and it gives minorities a feeling they have an opportunity.

It's true that there have been cases of sham interviews, but I know for a fact Dan Rooney called out, challenged and ultimately championed a change that is the spirit of the Rooney Rule. When I get frustrated because people are not abiding by the process, having the rule and having it named after him is, to me, a source of hope and strength because it speaks to the character of Dan Rooney.

Most of my adult life has been spent with the Steelers and the Rooney family. I was especially glad to hear that Jim Rooney was writing this book. Whenever the Ambassador had a "big dude" in town—a CEO, an Irish diplomat or the president of the United States, Jim was by his side. I know when speaking to those with influence, the Ambassador was always holding up the point of view of those without a say, whether it was minorities, small markets or the "guy on the street." Jim was the guy who was with him. Hearing from those perspectives will be one thing I look forward to in this story.

Finally, there's a short list of people who have helped the National Football League live up to its creed: To honor everyone, the fans, the players and all the teams. Dan Rooney was one of those people. And he was like that in all the other roles he played, as a father, a business leader, a philanthropist and a peacemaker.

Everywhere Dan Rooney went, he was revered. And this book will tell you why.

NOTE TO READER

BY JIM ROONEY

MY FATHER SPENT MUCH OF HIS PROFESSIONAL LIFE NAVIGATING THE DIFFERENCES BETWEEN DISPARATE PARTIES, trying to narrow the chasms that divided them. I wrote this book because I wanted to provide a story of a unique approach to leadership, management and organizational culture. I hope it will inspire the next generation of leaders.

In the book, I refer to my father with different monikers: my father, Dan, Dan Rooney, Ambassador Rooney and Rooney. These names took on different meanings depending on the storyteller. I decided to use all of them.

Most books written by an offspring fall into one of two categories: A Tell-all or a Beatification. In a lot of ways, this book falls into the latter. It didn't start that way, but the hundreds of hours I spent interviewing individuals transformed it into this. A book of gratitude. A book about revisiting my father's decisions and seeing the effectiveness in them.

Examining a 70-year-long career through all of these conversations with others could lead to unraveling stories I didn't want to hear. But my interviews with others were nothing but positive, and I take everyone at his or her word. There is no reason for those interviewed to be disingenuous. A dishonest assessment of my father could compromise the credibility of my interviewees—all of whom have motivation to protect professional reputations as business people, public figures or journalists.

The book outlines my father's approach as it played out in four major efforts of his life. This focus includes the Rooney Rule, the NFL policy that a diverse slate (at least one minority candidate is interviewed) be considered when hiring a head coach and general manager. It also includes his work throughout the peace process in Ireland and his work as a trustee of the NFL—with a particular emphasis on being the voice of reason in many of its most challenging negotiations. I also discuss my father's design and development of the Pittsburgh Steelers, transforming them from one of the most-inept organizations in sports history into one of the gold standards for stability and excellence within the sports-entertainment industry. I focus mainly on these endeavors because I believe they were transformational to the outcomes of these organizations as well as to the communities in which they functioned.

In focusing on just these four areas of my father's career, this book had to leave out many people who worked with him and supported so many different efforts of his. For Steelers fans, this includes Bill Cowher. He and my father had a tremendous working relationship. His contribution to the Steelers organization and fans was immense. But this book is not a chronology of Steelers history. Nevertheless, I certainly hope Steelers fans enjoy it and get a chance to see the inner workings of my father's approach. This approach did have such an impact on the team, while telling the story of his most transformational work.

Distilling my father's career into succinct themes was a challenge, but I narrowed it down to a few main ones:

- Playing the long game
- Doing the right thing
- Finding a measured and balanced approach in his work

They say good books describe conflict. The most fundamental internal challenge that I saw my father face was his constant struggle with wealth and money. He was never comfortable with the amount of wealth that he personally gained. And even more so, he felt the largest impediment to long-term success was in regard to the willingness of those involved to continue to strive for the highest levels of excellence once wealth was achieved.

In writing the book, I also wanted to show that success is about people being part of a team, finding ways to support the person next to them, and being willing to make sacrifices for one another in pursuit of a common goal. These qualities truly represent what is best about a team.

Finally, it's my hope that I demonstrate he was able to win while also being a "good guy"—and that such a unique approach to winning can make an authentic and long-lasting difference. I believe this approach to winning is more effective and delivers more sustainable results than the common view of winner take all.

STORY I | STEWARD:

FAITH, FAMILY, FOOTBALL

Nobody would have predicted that the National Football League would become an iconic global behemoth when it was created a century ago. The league struggled to find its footing in the 1920s, as baseball emerged as America's pastime. Then came the Depression, when businesses failed and millions were out of work and hungry. And yet the league did something extraordinary during those hardest of times—it saw an opportunity to expand. At that point my grandfather, Art Rooney, founded a new team called the Pittsburgh Pirates in 1933.

He paid $2,500 for the franchise at a time when Pennsylvania's blue laws banned the playing of football—and other games—on Sunday. There was no business plan. The Pirates played at Forbes Field, the home of the other Pittsburgh Pirates, the city's baseball team. The most expensive ticket was under $2 (around $38 today). Average attendance was below 12,000.

Young Dan, my father, was a year old when my grandfather founded the team. He would become part of the organization as a child, when he served as a ball boy. He became more involved in the team and the league as a young adult in the 1950s, just as the NFL was becoming the gold standard in sports business and management. But there was nothing inevitable about that growth: It required vision and an appreciation of how to play the long game.

As the NFL transformed itself in the 1960s, he insisted that the league maintain a meaningful connection to those who made that growth possible—the fans and the players. He was also a realist who understood that the NFL was a business. He fought hard for critical infrastructure and processes that were sound, visionary and viable. When he was at his best, the considerations of the business, the fans and the players were balanced.

Throughout his years in the NFL, my father believed it was possible to engage in give-and-take while maintaining one's integrity and another person's dignity.

ONE

BEGINNINGS

DANIEL MILTON ROONEY, first-born child of Art and Kathleen Rooney, was a business executive, a sports-team owner, a philanthropist and a diplomat. He had a long and memorable career, one that would seem to defy a simple description. But if you were to choose one word to describe who he was and how he carried himself no matter the setting, that word would have to be authenticity. He was who he was, and he didn't try to be what he wasn't. People respected that, and some even loved him for it. He didn't play the role of Dan Rooney. He was Dan Rooney.

Whether he was negotiating contracts in the NFL's board rooms, seeking and encouraging talent in places others overlooked, starting up a global charity or prodding longtime enemies to talk through their differences, my father never lost sight of who he was, what his values were and how to treat people—even those with whom he disagreed. He left behind a legacy that changed how we provide opportunity to those to whom it had been denied.

He was born in Pittsburgh's Mercy Hospital on July 20, 1932, and so became the first member of his family who wasn't born at home. He was assigned his role in life at the very moment of his birth. Dan was the first-born son, and in the Rooney family and in millions of other families, birth order and gender meant everything. As the first-born son of a striving, upwardly mobile family, my father would inherit not only the business but also the responsibilities that came with Art Rooney's legacy. Art was the Rooney who made it—not with a business plan, but through talent, guile, determination—and who tried to bring along as many Rooneys as he could. My father, as his first-born son, would have to figure out how to manage it all.

It would take a different skill set and different perspective: Art was the gregarious Irish uncle who, in later years, handed out Super Bowl tickets to any and all who asked, and many did. Dan Rooney was, figuratively speaking, the stern bookkeeper—he did study accounting at Duquesne University—who felt he had no choice but to bring order to what seemed to be a seat-of-the-pants operation. Part of that obsession with stability and continuity, I think, was the inevitable result of growing up during the Depression. But some of it was part of his Rooney DNA, a response to his assigned role. He was expected to be responsible and accountable, to be the one to whom others would turn for guidance and help, and the one to impose tough love if that was required.

Primogeniture, then, made him who he was and drove him to make the kinds of decisions he did. He didn't seek responsibility; it was his at birth, whether he liked it or not.

His father—soon to be known as "The Chief"—already was something of a legend in western Pennsylvania, a terrific, multi-talented athlete who excelled in baseball, football and boxing. Art Rooney was one of nine children (including one girl who died as a child of whooping cough) whose father, Daniel, disappeared from their lives for several years when Art was a toddler. Daniel's own father was an ironworker who died at 53, exhausted before his time, like so many others who worked in the mills and factories of industrializing America. They were immigrants or the children and grandchildren of immigrants, and in the case of the Rooneys, there was the unspoken but ever-present fear of the unknown and a yearning for security and stability. They carried unspoken memories of the hunger and deprivation suffered by their ancestor James Rooney, who fled Ireland in 1847, the height of the horrendous famine.

Hunger taught the Irish—those who remained in Ireland, and those who set sail across the Atlantic—new ways to find security and stability. If they relied on things they couldn't control—the weather, the potato, the land itself—they could die. When they came to America, they did not become farmers, as they had been in Ireland. Instead, they took jobs in the firehouses and coal mines and steel mills, which seemed to offer more stability than tending crops, or they sought to go into business for themselves in hopes of taking better control of their own fortunes.

For many, those memories of hunger and that fear of disorder led to unhappiness, dysfunction, alcoholism and depression. Not every immigrant story ends in stability and achievement. But nobody talked about the problems of those left behind—nobody even acknowledged that there was a problem. My father saw the pain firsthand, and it drove him to succeed, to take responsibility for his own life and the lives of those he could help. And like so many Irish-Americans, he could never shake the feeling that even—especially—in good times, disaster lurked just around the corner. You had to be prepared for the worst, he believed, and not lose sight of reality when things appear to be going well.

In 1899, Daniel Rooney, my great-grandfather, married 18-year-old Margaret Murray, the daughter of a coal miner. The young couple operated a series of mom-and-pop hotels and saloons, catering to coal miners and steelworkers in the industrial towns, and later in what is now Pittsburgh's North Side. They started a family, beginning with my grandfather's birth in 1901. But soon the family's finances collapsed as creditors came calling. Art's father disappeared, heading west to escape his financial burdens and leaving behind his pregnant wife and two small sons. He returned several years later and went back to work running a hotel and saloon, but in the interim, my great-grandmother, her mother-in-law and other formidable Rooney women kept the family together, providing stability and continuity in the face of an unexpected disaster.

Art soon began to make his mark on the world through sports and, later, local politics—two avenues the Irish used to get ahead in the early 20th century. He was a star baseball player at Duquesne University's prep school and for semipro teams in the local sandlots, and a top-notch boxer who defeated 1920 Olympic gold medalist Sammy Mosberg. By the 1920s, he and his brothers Dan and Jim were legends of western Pennsylvania's gridirons—Art played against Jim Thorpe and the Canton Bulldogs during his years in semipro football.

The passage of Prohibition destroyed the family business model, forcing Art's dad to shut the saloon that not only provided a livelihood but also made him a neighborhood celebrity and power broker. In a biography of my grandfather, writers Rob Ruck, Maggie Jones Patterson and Michael P. Weber argued that Daniel Rooney was never the same after his saloon on the North Side closed. They note that he was "prone to melancholy" already. The loss of his core business made matters worse.

In the late 1920s, my grandfather fell for a young woman named Kathleen McNulty, and she for him. But her father had other ideas for his daughter's future, and they didn't involve a son-in-law mixed up with football players and gamblers. So, in June 1931, my grandparents took a train to New York and were married in a civil ceremony there. It was a shocking thing to do, especially for two devout Catholics, but they wouldn't be denied.

Art was 31 years old when Dan was born, about a year after the scandalous ceremony in New York. He still was fit and strong, but it was time to find the kind of stability that the sandlot and the boxing ring couldn't provide. It was a hard time, though, to be starting something new, whether it was a business or a family.

The Great Depression was a foundational experience for anyone born in the 1930s, as both of my parents were. Memories of the insecurity and fear of those hard times never quite faded, no matter where they lived and, for the most part, no matter their circumstances.

For the first few years of his life, my father lived with his parents (and incoming Rooneys, for he quickly had four brothers: Art Jr., Timothy and twins Patrick and John) in an apartment above a furniture store in the North Side section of Pittsburgh.

My mother, Patricia, grew up nearby—they attended the same grade school on the North Side—and the struggles of her family shaped both of them for the rest of their lives.

My mother's father was a construction worker, a union man, and, like most families, their welfare depended on the availability of jobs. If my mom's dad got a steady job, things were good. But there were times when he had no job at all and her family could afford little. Her mother always figured out how to get her family fed, but often it was just soup. Sometimes they went to the convent, where they were given bread and other necessities. It was a constant struggle to come up with the money for a serving of milk at school. There were visits to the gas company to plead for a few extra days to pay the bill before the gas would be turned off.

As soon as they were old enough, my mom and her older brother got jobs—my mom worked at a local drugstore and then at a Woolworth's—to help support their family. They tried to make money so that their younger siblings could have things for Easter and Christmas. My mother still says proudly that the younger kids never realized how fragile the family's situation was.

There was no escaping the sights and sounds of hopelessness, even after my father's family moved to a larger house a block away, on North Lincoln Avenue. One day during the depths of the Depression, a strange man knocked on the door as young Dan watched from a bedroom window. The stranger was hungry and asked my grandmother for food. She told him to come around to the back door, where she brought out a plate and handed him a few dollars. Decades later, Dan remembered the scene as if it had happened the day before. "I'll always remember the face of real hunger," he wrote, "and the value of charity."

Elsewhere on the North Side, groups of unemployed men set up shanty towns in open spaces and parks, or became squatters in abandoned storefronts. Even North Siders who were lucky enough to have jobs and homes understood that so many neighbors, through no fault of their own, were hungry and homeless, living off the kindness of strangers, and sometimes relying on that kindness even after death. My grandfather sometimes paid for the funerals of his neighbors, which ensured that their families and friends could accompany the bodies of loved ones to distant cemeteries.

Through his boxing promotion business, my grandfather dominated the Pittsburgh boxing scene, with his fights drawing crowds of fans that ranged from priests and politicians to steelworkers and thugs. Boxing made money.

Football did not. My grandfather had purchased one of the semipro teams he had played on, and he founded a new regional football organization, the West

Penn Conference, less than a year after the stock market crash of 1929. He invited a well-known barnstorming team of African-American players (there were few opportunities for African-American players then in the nascent NFL) led by the legendary Fritz Pollard to play his own team. The conference failed as a business, but by then my grandfather had set his sights even higher: He wanted to bring a National Football League franchise to Pittsburgh.

The NFL in 1932 was preparing to do something few other businesses would dare try in the depths of the Depression: It was looking to expand, even after several false starts in the 1920s and failures during the Depression cut the number of teams from 22 in 1926 to just eight in 1932. Franchises in the country's major markets now dominated the league: Three teams were in New York City (the Giants, the Brooklyn Dodgers and the Staten Island Stapletons), and two were in Chicago (the Bears and the Cardinals). The other teams were in Boston, Green Bay and Portsmouth, Ohio.

In the summer of 1933, not long after Dan's first birthday, Art Rooney paid the NFL $2,500 for the right to establish a new team—the Pittsburgh Pirates. Two other franchises joined the league that summer: the Philadelphia Eagles, owned by future NFL commissioner Bert Bell, and the Cincinnati Reds.

The founding of the team was really that simple. There was no business plan, only my grandfather's instincts. And there certainly were no grand expectations. My grandfather could never have imagined the NFL would explode into the business and wellspring of passion it has become. Even Dan Rooney did not envision the NFL as the cultural force and the extraordinary revenue generator it is now.

The concern for the team during those early days after its founding—and even into the 1950s, when Dan was getting involved—was keeping it going from year to year. After six seasons, my grandfather's NFL deficit was more than $100,000. Well after the nation's economy had recovered and the NFL began to create a stronger foothold in America's leisure time, remaining competitive as a small market team against larger market teams that could earn and spend much more on players was an animating concern for my dad. And it informed his thinking for years afterward.

When my grandfather started the team, it was not his biggest business and he likely never thought it would be. He had been successful in other businesses, though, and my father watched as several close family members lived beyond their means and struggled with the trappings of relative wealth, which they came to enjoy because my grandfather was bankrolling them.

Dan Rooney was certainly not poor and he did not live in a monastery. He owned a plane to fulfill his passion for flying. And owning an NFL team is an undeniable and exalted fruit of American privilege. But he lived about as minimalist and disciplined a life as anyone in his role could. There were no vacation homes, and family travel was rooted in education—whether about Ireland or the journey of Lewis and Clark. He constantly lectured his children about not putting on airs. My mother gently still jokes that she's not sure all of us got the message.

We children often teased our father about his very plain and often old clothes. We would spot a picture of him in a magazine and joke that someone had to make sure he never wore a particular suit again. Players volunteered to take him shopping. Every Sunday night, he took out his two big pairs of black shoes and one pair of brown shoes and polished them himself. He drove a Pontiac Bonneville. (He was a fast and aggressive driver, to the dismay of some of his family.) Until fairly late in life, he would walk home up the hill after games—our family home is about a 10-minute walk from the stadium on the North Side—with all the other fans heading out. Only in his last decade did he have a security person with him, at the insistence of his children. On the night before the Steelers played in Super Bowl XXX in Tempe, Arizona, most of the Steelers' contingent attended a glitzy NFL party and he teased us about going to a "rich dudes" party. My parents got in their rented Ford and drove to a nearby Denny's, because, my father said, he wanted to eat "something normal" the night before the game.

He warned us, "Don't make money your god. If you believe money is going to make your life easier and solve your problems, you're wrong. It's education. That will determine if you are happy, if you're successful."

He would say, "I don't care if you're a garbageman. Be great at that."

My father didn't mind making money. He didn't mind players having money.

He minded—maybe he was overly obsessive about it, especially late in his life—the love of money. That concern about the corrupting power of money and how it affected the things he cared about—his family, the players, the NFL—shaped not only how he lived his own life, but also how he approached business.

Real-world concerns like those that frequently occupied my dad had, in fact, always been a strong undercurrent of the league.

From its very earliest days, the NFL has reflected the country, its breakthroughs and struggles, for better or worse. The team my grandfather founded was no different.

The original roster of the Pirates included Ray Kemp, a black guard from Duquesne University. He was one of just two black players in the league in 1933. Joe Lillard, a running back for the Chicago Cardinals, was the other. Both were gone by the end of that season. Kemp left to become a coach, and he had a long and successful career.

But after that first season, my grandfather, in the one glaring mistake of his career, did not challenge the unofficial agreement among NFL owners to ban black players. Some owners like Washington's George Preston Marshall were openly hostile to black players, while tolerating players from other ethnic minorities, including Native Americans.

We were no different from, and certainly no better than, the rest of the country. The desperation generated by the Great Depression had undoubtedly given rise to an increase in racism. Segregation was the norm. Diminished or nonexistent opportunities for minorities were standard and were accepted without much thought. It would be more than a decade before the NFL would have another black player, when Kenny Washington signed with the Los Angeles Rams in 1946. The Steelers would not have another black player until we drafted fullback Jack Spinks from Alcorn State in the 11th round in 1952.

That long detachment from black players was a marked incongruity for my grandfather, who otherwise had a history of working with the black sports communities in baseball and boxing.

My grandfather collaborated with the founders and leaders of the two Negro league baseball teams in Pittsburgh, the Homestead Grays and the Pittsburgh Crawfords. Cumberland Posey, the founder of the Grays, went to Duquesne with my grandfather and had a significant influence on his life and, by extension, on my father's. Posey, an African-American pioneer in college sports, is the only person elected to both the basketball and baseball halls of fame. He was a star senior when my grandfather arrived on campus. Posey took my grandfather under his wing. The friendship lasted the rest of their lives. When Posey needed seed money so the Grays could go to spring training—which meant playing in the South, where they could raise operating funds—he would get the money from my grandfather.

My grandfather's boxing promotion company was one of the best known in the country in an era when boxing was one of the top sports. At that time, black fighters were routinely denied top billing on cards in other cities, but my grandfather's matches regularly featured black boxers. In 1951, my grandfather promoted a bout between Jersey Joe Walcott and Ezzard Charles, the first time in history two black men boxed for an open heavyweight championship belt. My grandfather's open-minded contribution to baseball and boxing doesn't excuse his approach to the struggling NFL, but it certainly demonstrates the lack of importance the league held for him in those days.

My father grew up watching my grandfather's relationship with the black community and it undoubtedly shaped his own relationships. At the same time, my grandfather was preparing his oldest son for the job he was groomed for since childhood, when he was the Steelers' water boy at training camp. While still in college in the early 1950s, Dan Rooney joined the Steelers management, first as a training camp manager—he arranged schedules and wrote the checks for the laundry—and then as a contract negotiator. By the mid-1950s, he had assumed a greater role in team operations and was attending owners' meetings. He was managing the team, with his father's pointed advice ringing in his ears:

"Do it your way. But don't screw it up."

The truth was, by the time Dan got involved, he couldn't have made things much worse. My grandfather was a beloved local figure, so the Steelers bore the label of "lovable losers." But losers they were.

The Steelers were the league's doormat, with only nine winning seasons in 40 years. Pittsburgh was a baseball town then and the Steelers' performance did nothing to change that. They had long losing streaks, including 13 losses in a row at home from December 1944 to December 1945 and then 16 consecutive home losses from September 1969 to October 1970.

The devotion of Steelers fans that exists now was nowhere to be found then, for good reason. From 1933 to 1945, average attendance was just 15,250—less than half of Forbes Field's capacity. As the NFL grew in popularity, other teams saw attendance soar—the average was 43,617 in 1959. But the Steelers averaged just 26,645 that year.

There was one embarrassment after another. In 1944, the Steelers partnered with my grandfather's best friend in football, Charles Bidwill and the Chicago Cardinals (they are now based in Arizona). The reason: The teams wanted to try to economize during the lean years of World War II. The result was a team as laughable as its name: Card-Pitts. It was, arguably, the worst team in NFL history. Card-Pitts lost every game and fined players for indifferent play. Tellingly, the best player on the team quit football completely. Is it any surprise that Card-Pitts quickly morphed to "Carpets" among the local writers?

Things were no better off the field. In the 1950s, the official vehicle of the Steelers was an Oldsmobile station wagon. The dealer who provided the cars was certainly not worried about giving the team his best models.

For instance, the car my father drove would not go uphill while in drive.

That was especially bad news considering the team played then at Pitt Stadium, which sat on a hill about 500 feet from the main thoroughfare through campus, Fifth Avenue. For each home game, my father would pull past the turnoff for the stadium's drive, put the car in reverse and then drive—backward—up the hill. My sisters, then preteens, ducked under the windows to avoid the humiliation of being seen in the car going in reverse all the way up the hill. Especially because there was no missing who was in it. That car bore an "Official Car of the Pittsburgh Steelers" logo painted on its side.

More than a decade before he reshaped the Steelers, most of a lifetime before he became a U.S. ambassador, Dan Rooney was known around the NFL simply as "the kid," still very much in the shadow of his father, particularly in the eyes of other team owners. As the Chief's eldest son, it was always known that Dan would eventually run the Steelers, so his apprenticeship started early. But he was still younger than most of the people in the NFL.

Just a few years out of school, married, starting a family and working in the team's personnel department during the 1950s, Dan forged an early friendship with a young public relations specialist who would later become the general manager of the Los Angeles Rams.

My father and Pete Rozelle were close in age—Rozelle was six years Rooney's senior—and alike in temperament. They were quiet, preferring one-on-one conversations. In group settings, they were happy to let others talk before weighing in. During the late 1950s, they worked together on early marketing projects for the league. It was the beginning of a partnership that extended for more than 30 years and which was threaded through some of the most momentous decisions in NFL history.

When NFL commissioner Bert Bell died in October 1959 after suffering a heart attack while watching a game between the Eagles and Steelers—Bell had at different times held ownership stakes in both of those teams—the league lost one of its great pioneers at the age of 64. The loss created an unanticipated vacuum of power at the very top of the league at a particularly important time. Bell had led the NFL since 1945, but societal changes—Americans were moving to the suburbs and tuning into televisions—were sure to impact the NFL. Choosing a commissioner who could lead the league into the future figured to be a daunting task.

It was certainly that.

Two Georges—Halas in Chicago and Preston Marshall in Washington—were the most significant, domineering voices in any NFL meeting room. As a result, a cluster of other owners did not want a commissioner who would simply be beholden to their outsize influence.

When Rozelle's name was raised as a possible candidate, my grandfather asked my dad what he knew about him. Dan told him that Rozelle was bright and talented, and that while he was a little young—Rozelle was 33 at the time— he was someone they could work with.

Ultimately, Rozelle won the support of a coalition of owners that Bell had occasionally cobbled together to counter the influence of Halas and Marshall. This coalition was an early indicator of the alliance between small and large market teams on which the modern league would be built. The representatives of the Steelers, Green Bay Packers, New York Giants, Chicago Cardinals and Los Angeles Rams did not agree on everything. But here they came together to make Rozelle the commissioner three months after Bell died. And Dan became, as Joe Browne, who spent 50 years as a league executive in public and government relations, put it, "Pete's right arm."

Rozelle was the first of three commissioners with whom Dan Rooney worked closely as a "whip"—coalescing support among his fellow owners—confidant and, later in his life, a mentor. From the beginning, Rooney thought that the NFL needed a strong commissioner and a strong league office, whose business would be to make decisions that benefited the entire league—players, clubs and fans—not just a few powerful owners. That attitude still sometimes causes flare-ups within the league, because there have always been and will probably always be owners who don't want people they employ at the league office, including the commissioner, to accrue too much power and tell them what to do. But Dan Rooney was one of the owners—the Giants' Wellington Mara, with whom Dan was close, was another—who would try to sell other owners on the direction coming from the commissioner's office. As a result, he spent a lot of time on the phone with owners. Most nights at home, he had at least one or two phone calls with other owners or the commissioner.

That role was as crucial as anything else my father did in the NFL. As much as Rozelle—and later Paul Tagliabue—relied on my father and Wellington Mara, they were only two votes. No matter how great his vision, my father simply could not have gotten anything done without the input and leadership of other owners. The NFL's system is not set up for those who want to go it alone. Most substantive changes made to the league—from rules changes to team relocations—require 75 percent of owners to vote in favor. In the current league of 32 teams, that means 24 owners must be on the same side, placing a premium on negotiation, compromise, teamwork and persuasion. My father had a lot of big-picture ideas about the NFL, but he was above all a realist. When the NFL was confronting issues, that meant positioning himself as a source of compromise, so he could work closely with a number of other owners to forge consensus.

Rozelle needed the help. In the 1960s, the NFL staff was small, numbering just a handful of people, far from the sprawling operation based on Park Avenue in midtown Manhattan today. He and Dan, who had not yet taken over day-to-day control of the Steelers, spoke regularly. Dan Rooney became an extension of the staff, taking on projects at Rozelle's behest.

It was a good fit. Dan Rooney was an early believer in Rozelle's vision for the league and had a gift for envisioning projects from start to finish. When Rozelle took over, baseball was still very much the national pastime and the NFL was still searching for its niche in American culture. Rozelle, more so than his predecessors, knew that teams would have to work together as a league to build something, particularly on television deals. My brother Art believes our father and grandfather shared that understanding but that Dan's relationship with Rozelle strengthened his core business principle of taking the long view, that there would be times he would have to forgo opportunities that would be best for the Steelers in order to get a bigger gain down the road for the entire NFL. And that it was better to be fair to all sides in a negotiation than to extract that last bit of benefit and leave the other party aggrieved.

My father had a temper, although it showed itself only in brief, relatively mild, bursts. Still, it was an enduring source of frustration for him when others didn't share the same long-range approach and the same pursuit of the collective good.

"That was his way of saying a person wasn't getting the message. He would say, 'They don't look at the big picture,' " my mother, Patricia, said. "That was very important to him. He saw his dad and it was a tough beginning for the National Football League. As things grew and everything got more manageable, he could see that you could go beyond what the Chief was doing. He could see openings, possibilities. He would get really upset about someone's decision—he would say, 'They just don't see the big picture.' "

Dan Rooney believed deeply that football could act as a unifier, as a way to form fundamental connections, as a force for good. To start up a conversation with someone he did not know, he would invariably draw them out by asking about their favorite team. He loved kidding friends from Cleveland and Baltimore—the Steelers' division rivals—about their teams. He understood the outsize role he eventually had at the top level of NFL decision-making, but during those conversations, he was like every other guy at a sports bar.

That desire for unity and consensus—and concern for the fans—shaped so much of how he approached the business of the NFL.

All of those phone calls with owners were about cajoling, explaining and twisting arms to get everybody to work in concert. Dan Rooney never held an elected public office. But he was a master at the politics of the league, and he loved being at the center of the action that led to the growth of the NFL.

"He was willing to serve as an ambassador for the league," Browne said. "We've had owners over the years who enjoyed being NFL owners a little too much. They want to build up their own personal brand so they can take it elsewhere for financial gain. Dan and his dad were not like that. Dan was willing to do things because it was what was right. It was such a different time. The league was struggling to make this thing work. Now, it almost seems like it is turnkey. In those days, it was far from turnkey."

Early struggles, personal and professional, likely played some role in my father's unusual (at least among team owners) ambivalence toward the business's holy grail: He thought the lust for money weakened and corrupted most people.

As mentioned earlier, Dan Rooney essentially believed greed was the root of all human problems. And he thought all of us—players, owners, the families—got seduced by money. His fear and concern for individuals and for the league was that we would lose our way because we would make corrupting or lazy compromises, that we would be looking for the more comfortable way rather than for the right way.

Nobody was making all that much money from football when the league first began in 1920 as a group of 14 teams, most of them in the Midwest. Even well into the 1950s, around the time Dan was first getting involved with the Steelers' operations and was forging a friendship with the man who would become the next commissioner, it was a minor player compared to Major League Baseball, college football and boxing.

But just as the NFL was trying to find its niche, another new business was alighting on American culture—television. The symbiotic relationship between TV and the NFL—and the way the NFL has managed and maximized the revenue that has flowed from it—remains the single greatest driver of the league's popularity and fortune.

From the start, football seemed designed to flourish on a small screen. The rectangular field fit neatly into a television set's dimensions. The stoppages in play allowed for regularly spaced commercials. The predictable length of games suited network programmers. Even the equipment and uniforms—the helmets and face masks and shoulder pads—created a mystique that enhanced the drama.

The very first NFL game to be televised—between the Philadelphia Eagles and Brooklyn Dodgers—took place in 1939, reaching approximately 1,000 television sets in the New York City area. Throughout the 1940s, coverage was sporadic. But in 1953, as Americans were buying homes and televisions to furnish them during the post-World War II boom, the DuMont network created the first regularly scheduled NFL program, at 8 p.m. on Saturdays. A few individual teams had their own deals and even had the foresight to create their own networks, but the DuMont program was the forerunner to the national television packages we have today.

The Steelers played the New York Giants in the first game on DuMont (the Steelers won, 24–14), but made only occasional money from television during the 1950s.

Rooney always believed that cost management was the most critical aspect of financial success. Until the end of his life, he was uncomfortable with borrowing and carrying significant debt.

So it was an enduring irony of Dan Rooney's life: The man who feared the temptations of great wealth played a significant role in developing the mechanisms that led to the explosion of NFL revenue from its two most important sources, television and stadiums.

Rozelle, who was born one year before the first electronic television was invented in 1927, understood better than anyone in the league that the television partnership with a national audience, coupled with a plan to share the revenue among teams, was critical for the NFL to grow. By the late 1930s, televisions were being sold to the public and they were an instant success. Rozelle was growing up professionally just as television was growing up, first as the public relations manager for the Los Angeles Rams in the early 1950s, and later as the team's general manager. It was not a coincidence that Rozelle worked for the first team to televise its home games.

But like some other longtime league stewards, Dan Rooney harbored concerns about television's potential impact on the game. It was, in part, related to his larger belief that too much money could become too controlling. He worried that once television and the NFL had a relationship, television would become so powerful that the desires of the industry—for instance, for commercial breaks—would impact decisions made about the game. Would fans sit through commercial breaks if they lasted too long? Would the widespread availability of games on television keep fans from going to stadiums?

They probably worried too much about those details. A lot of people have enjoyed a lot of football on television in all these years and it is impossible to imagine either the game or the medium without the other. Those early concerns, though, about television's ability to influence decisions about the direction of the league—and about what the league must do to draw fans into stadiums and away from their televisions—are as relevant today as they were when Rozelle and the NFL were first grappling with them.

Still, after making only occasional money from television throughout the 1950s, Rooney knew the Steelers had to approach it more systematically as the decade was drawing to a close. There had been fewer than 10 million television sets in American homes in 1950. By 1959, there were more than 67 million. If the Steelers were going to survive and remain competitive, they could not afford to miss out on the riches that were flowing to others.

In 1959, my father and grandfather met with Carroll Rosenbloom, then the owner of the Baltimore Colts, and Tom Galley of NBC. CBS owned most of the NFL's television packages. NBC wanted in and Galley was proposing a weekly broadcast alternating between Pittsburgh and Baltimore games.

The Steelers were coming off three relatively successful seasons—a rarity for them at that time—and the Colts won the championship in 1958 and 1959. They had Pittsburgh native Johnny Unitas at quarterback and had played in the 1958 NFL championship game, which they won in overtime over the Giants in Yankee Stadium, considered by many to be the greatest game ever played.

NBC offered a $900,000 contract for the first season. Rosenbloom said he had to get $575,000 out of the deal, which left $325,000 for the Steelers. My grandfather glared at him and said, "I thought we were partners."

My father and grandfather, angered by what they considered to be Rosenbloom's bullying, stepped out of the room.

"Forget it, let's get out of here," Dan said to my grandfather. "This bum is taking advantage of us. I wouldn't let him do this."

But my grandfather had already calmed down. He knew of the Steelers' financial woes over the years. They'd made just $125,000 from television the previous season. His kindness sometimes got in the way of business realities and he may occasionally even have been taken advantage of. But he persuaded my father it made sense to make this deal, which gave the Steelers their first major television contract.

And it gave Dan Rooney insight into two crucial points for the future of the NFL—how television viewed the appeal of the game, and how important the right split among teams would be.

Rozelle was moving into the commissioner's office at around the same time and he was facing twin challenges—how to build a strategic approach to television, and how to fend off a fledgling rival league, the American Football League, which had eight teams then and had signed a league-wide television deal with ABC. The competition from the AFL would be the motivator for the NFL to give television the attention it demanded and deserved.

Rozelle based his strategy on three pillars. He wanted a blackout rule to protect attendance at games. He wanted teams to have a plan to share the revenue, rather than have teams establishing individual deals for themselves. He understood that teams in New York, Los Angeles, Philadelphia and Chicago—which had significantly larger populations and more television owners—would have enjoyed mammoth revenue advantages over their smaller-market brethren. And he wanted a league-wide television partnership, because he recognized that competing with the AFL and building the prosperity of the NFL would require a national audience.

Getting everybody to go along took some work and that was clear from the very beginning. At the same meeting in Miami during which Rozelle was elected commissioner in 1960, Dan Rooney and Dan Reeves, the owner of the Los Angeles Rams, got into a heated discussion. Reeves felt that for a package television deal to work, the larger markets deserved a bigger piece of the pie. Rooney, with the negotiations with NBC still fresh in his mind and cognizant that Pittsburgh could never generate as much money as a team in Los Angeles, thought the only fair way to divide the money was evenly. He believed that the national presence for football—as opposed to the local and regional deals that Major League Baseball relied on—would eventually provide exponential growth for all teams. The large market teams were taking on more of the early risk, though, because they would have been able to count on more money from a local television contract. While the smaller market teams would initially be favored by an equal revenue sharing plan, Dan Rooney believed that, in time, everyone would benefit.

As the argument continued, Reeves told Rooney that he would never get enough votes from team owners to implement an equal revenue sharing system.

"What would you do about it?" Reeves challenged.

Rooney replied: "Well, when you come to Pittsburgh, there aren't going to be any Los Angeles Rams games broadcast back to L.A. We have every right in the world to do this."

Reeves: "Then you won't get any money."

Rooney: "Then neither will you."

Not long after, at the 1961 league meeting, Rozelle presented his television plan that would form the foundation of the NFL's future. My father and grandfather were enlisted to work alongside Vince Lombardi from Green Bay (a former Giants assistant coach and a Fordham University classmate of Wellington Mara) to persuade their lifelong friends—the Maras of the New York Giants—to commit to some version of shared revenue. No decision would be as pivotal as the one made by the Maras because no team would have reaped more benefits from keeping their own television audience to themselves.

By then, big market teams like the Giants and Bears had all of their games on television. Smaller market teams like the Packers and 49ers did not. If the NFL hoped to have any semblance of competitive balance, the disparity in revenue—at the time, it was already more than $100,000 per year between the Giants and Packers—was not sustainable.

The Giants' founder, Tim Mara, and his sons Wellington and Jack were considered, even more than the Rooneys, "league men," devoted to putting the interests of the NFL ahead of their own. Tim Mara, who died in 1959, was one of my grandfather's closest friends, and their teams remain so intertwined that, to this day, John Mara, Tim Mara's grandson and the president of the Giants, and my brother Art sit beside each other at owners' meetings, just as their fathers did. In fact, the families are more than intertwined—they're related. Kathleen Rooney, another of Art's grandchildren, is married to Chris Mara, Wellington's son.

But the conversation about television revenue was tense.

At one point, Jack questioned my grandfather's Catholicism, calling him a thief for "stealing" money that rightfully would have been generated by New York. My grandfather was incensed, demanding that Mara never again question his religion. My father thought he might have to jump between them, calculating that my grandfather, though 15 years older than Jack Mara, would have been the prohibitive favorite because of his years in the boxing ring.

The Maras were no pushovers and neither was the Bears' George Halas. But the pitch from Rozelle, Lombardi and Dan Rooney was rooted in something that is now taken for granted about the appeal of the NFL: The league would only be as strong as its weakest link and unequal distribution of television money would create just a few very strong links—teams with much greater resources, which would have given them a huge leg up in signing players—and many more weak teams. And that would, in time, lessen the appeal for fans and doom the entire league. These were business decisions, but they were rooted in something more emotional. Rooney and the other league decision-makers wanted to create something that people would grow to love, that they would enjoy for generations. For years later, Wellington Mara preached the importance of having a level playing field, even pointing to Major League Baseball, which has more liberal free agency than the NFL does, as an example of what the NFL did not want—a handful of teams that spent more always being near the top. That would be terrible for fans.

"They just felt you have to give fans in each city the same opportunity to win," said John Mara. "That's what creates a great league, where everybody has hope. In the short term, maybe there were things that would have been better for us. But I'm not sure in the long term, if you had teams that were noncompetitive, if that's the best thing for our sport going forward."

But there was another factor in Rozelle's favor when the revenue sharing decision was made: "The money wasn't that big then," Browne said. "Pete saw the impact of television, but some of the owners didn't. They were still back in the 1950s, thinking ticket revenue would always be the number one source of revenue. If they could have had a crystal ball and seen 30 years down, some of them may not have done it."

Fortunately for the NFL, the Maras did, and they ultimately agreed with equal sharing of television revenue. And because they owned the team in the biggest market, their voices became the most critical in persuading other large market franchises to support Rozelle's plan.

It was the most transformative moment in the history of the NFL. Rozelle was renowned for his smoothness, particularly in his dealings with television networks, sponsors and Congress. But it was his innate fairness that made him such a successful commissioner.

"I remember him saying with some degree of pride that when he did the television negotiations, he never tried to extract the last possible dollar," said Jeff Pash, the league's top lawyer, who came to know Rozelle when he was working for the league's law firm. "He tried to make a very good deal for the owners, but he wanted the networks to leave the negotiation feeling good as well and not feeling as though they had been squeezed to the point where they just had to get out of the room. Because he had the long-term view that, 'Hey, it's a continuing relationship.' "

That was a view Dan Rooney shared with Rozelle. Creating balance would be a cornerstone of Rooney's approach to business for more than 50 years.

The 1950s and 1960s were painful for the Steelers. They did not make the playoffs once in those two decades and had just four winning seasons. And they cycled through coaches at an alarming clip. Between 1950 and 1968, six different men led the Steelers, none of them with much success.

There was one event during that stretch that illustrated the problem.

The Steelers needed a new coach. They had just endured a 2-12 season under Mike Nixon, a former Steelers player who, as the Washington Redskins coach, had gone 4-16-2 in two seasons. Nixon had become the Steelers' head coach when Buddy Parker abruptly quit two weeks before the start of the 1965 season.

When the 1965 season came to a merciful conclusion, Nixon was fired. Rooney was immersed in his work for the league with Rozelle, but at the same time he was also taking on more responsibility with the Steelers. He was preparing to pivot the franchise into the future. He wanted to conduct a thorough coaching search—because he believed that taking the time to consider a wide range of candidates would help ensure the best person for long-term success would be chosen.

Dozens of people were considered. But Vince Lombardi, my grandfather's old pal and the legendary coach of the Green Bay Packers, had put in a good word for Bill Austin, one of his former assistant coaches. Austin got the job at my grandfather's insistence, and he publicly credited Lombardi's recommendation for the decision.

The Steelers often were not open-minded enough when making big decisions to rely on a disciplined, analytical process before coming to a conclusion.

That, and many other things, were about to change—on and off the field.

TWO

TRANSFORMATION

ON THE FIELD, THE 1960S BROUGHT ABOUT A TRANSFORMATION for the NFL as a business and as a cultural phenomenon.

The new American Football League began play in 1960 and became a thorn in the side of the NFL almost immediately. Lamar Hunt, an heir to an oil fortune, had tried and failed to acquire an NFL team in the late 1950s. So in August 1959, Hunt and other businessmen created their own league with eight teams including the Boston Patriots, Denver Broncos, New York Titans and Dallas Texans.

The NFL responded quickly. It put a team in Dallas—the Cowboys, in 1960— to counter Hunt's Dallas Texans. And in 1965, Dan Rooney was dispatched on one of Rozelle's projects. The prize was pro football in Atlanta. The AFL had already staged preseason games there earlier in the decade. A new venue, Atlanta-Fulton County Stadium, opened in 1965. But what made Atlanta so attractive was the television possibility. Atlanta was the major city in the Deep South and would command a region that would stretch, at that time, from Baltimore to Houston. The state's governor, Carl Sanders, wanted the NFL, although the AFL already seemed several steps ahead in establishing a presence there.

Dan Rooney's job was to identify who would be the best potential owner and then help sway him to pick the NFL over the AFL during a furious weeks-long period of lobbying by both leagues. My father spent a lot of time with Rankin

Smith, an insurance executive who was a close friend of the governor and whom the AFL had also approached.

Rooney was invited to play golf at the hallowed Augusta National with some people from Atlanta the NFL was trying to woo. While he appreciated the significance of the venue, golf was not exactly his passion.

"So he showed up at Augusta for this round of golf," my brother Art remembers. "He didn't even own golf shoes. He showed up wearing these coaching shoes. People were kind of making fun of him."

The venture was no laughing matter for Dan Rooney. The NFL realized the threat the AFL posed, and Atlanta became a key battleground in the war between the leagues. He and Rozelle were selling the NFL as the more established league. It had tradition. It had the positions in the largest markets in the country. There was more of a foundation to build on than with a start-up league like the AFL. Rozelle commissioned a survey by pollster Lou Harris to show that the NFL was the better candidate. The poll showed that Atlanta fans favored an NFL team by a 5-1 margin.

The AFL had already awarded a team to Smith, but the upstart league simply could not compete with the established popularity and the potential growth of the NFL, so Smith reneged. Because of Dan Rooney's leadership, the NFL had won the battle in Atlanta. On June 30, 1965, Smith—who admitted he knew nothing about football—was granted the right to pay $8.5 million for the expansion franchise.

That was the springboard for my father to spend much of his time on expansion as the league sought to broaden its footprint across the country. Before the expansion to Atlanta, the league was crowded into the Northeast and Midwest, the traditional population centers of the mid-20th century before interstate highways, suburbanization and deindustrialization changed the face of the country. He and Rozelle spent significant time trying to determine who would be good partners for the league—who had the financial wherewithal, certainly, to start and run a team, but also who would be good representatives of the NFL in their markets, striking the balance that was so important to Rooney.

Interest in the sport was booming. In the autumn of 1965, a Harris survey showed sports fans chose professional football as their favorite sport, overtaking baseball for the first time. But by then it was clear that the competition with the AFL couldn't go on—not for franchise locations, or television contracts or players—and that a merger offered the best chance for everybody to thrive. The dam finally burst when, in the spring of 1966, the Giants signed kicker Pete Gogolak away from the Buffalo Bills of the AFL. The move broke an unwritten agreement that neither league would raid the other's veteran players. Al Davis, the Oakland Raiders' coach and general manager who had recently taken over as AFL commissioner, encouraged retaliation—he wanted AFL teams to sign the NFL's quarterbacks. An all-out war for star players would have drained everbody's resources, even with those new television contracts. But Davis was—and remained—a renegade.

In June 1966, just a year after the two leagues had gone to war over Atlanta and shortly after Rozelle had launched secret negotiations—Hunt and the Cowboys' Tex Schramm would sit in a car at Dallas' Love Field so nobody would spot them—the AFL and NFL announced that they would merge, albeit slowly. Davis was furious that he had been excluded from the negotiations and quit after only a few months as the AFL commissioner, returning to the Raiders, where he emerged as the owner and general manager.

Even with the merger in the works, the competition between the two leagues was not fully relieved. Rooney said that Davis still treated NFL teams as the enemy—his relationship with Davis was almost always contentious—and even the newly created "Super Bowl" did nothing to unite the factions. The NFL teams believed their league was the superior one, creating immense pressure on their teams to beat the AFL counterparts for the world championship each year. Rozelle, who would become commissioner of the merged league, wanted the NFL to prevail in the Super Bowl, but he wanted the games to be competitive, to prove that a merger of the league would work.

He got half of his wish in the first two Super Bowls, when Lombardi's Green Bay Packers, one of the NFL's standard-bearer teams, bludgeoned their AFL opponents. For the inaugural game in 1967, they beat the Kansas City Chiefs by 25 points; the following year, they rolled over the Oakland Raiders by a margin of 19.

Then came Super Bowl III, when Joe Namath of the AFL's upstart New York Jets guaranteed a victory over the highly favored Baltimore Colts—and delivered. It is remembered now as a seminal moment for the league, but the NFL old guard was livid over the outcome. My father attended a postmortem dinner at a hotel in Miami after the game with Wellington Mara, Art Modell of the Cleveland Browns, Tex Schramm of the Dallas Cowboys and Lombardi. They vented their frustration. Rooney recalled hearing Lombardi criticizing Baltimore's coaching staff. That was ironic, because the next day, Dan was to interview Chuck Noll, who was on Don Shula's Colts staff, for a job with the Steelers. My father didn't necessarily share the anger of the rest of the group. He rarely got too high or too low after a game, even one as big as this.

Besides, he quietly agreed with Rozelle, who was disappointed but not crestfallen by Super Bowl III. The victory by the Jets may have embarrassed the NFL, but it proved that the leagues were on a level competitive field and that when the merger was finally complete, there would be balance.

It was, in gridiron form, the embodiment of Dan Rooney's focus on playing the long game. Sometimes you had to take a short-term loss to achieve a long-term victory. In the plan for the merged leagues, the Steelers were among the NFL teams that had to join AFL teams in the newly formed American Football Conference of the merged league. Rooney balked—he wanted to remain with the traditional teams of the NFL that would form the new National Football Conference of the merged league—but he finally acquiesced to Rozelle's wishes. Still, he was never fully convinced moving the Steelers to the AFC was best for the team.

"Dan said a number of times [and on different issues], 'I disagree with you, but I'll support you,'" Browne recalled of Dan Rooney's uneasy agreement to let the Steelers go to the AFC (for example) to finally settle the merged league's lineup. "I used to think he was kidding. But that's the way he was."

With the merged league to begin play in 1970, Rozelle wanted to create a television package of weekly Monday night games. Prime-time sports, taken for granted now, was unheard of then. Out of loyalty, Rozelle approached CBS first and they turned it down. NBC did not want to abandon its movie of the week, so they weren't interested. So Rozelle turned to ABC and producer Roone Arledge as the third choice.

The beauty of that deal, Rozelle told Browne often, was that the merged league was then on all three broadcast networks. And not just for games but during the week, the new NFL enjoyed the marketing power of all three networks.

How critical was success of the realigned league in settling the merger and the television contracts? In 1970, the first year of the merged league, television rights fees were $46.25 million, up from $4.65 million in that first contract just eight years earlier, when revenue sharing was first put in place. The league signed nine-year deals from 2014 to 2022 with its three broadcast partners (CBS, NBC, Fox) and ESPN for a combined total of $39.6 billion. The Associated Press reported that the television deal is worth approximately $5.66 billion annually through 2022. Nearly 55 years after that Harris survey noted its ascension, the NFL remains atop Americans' rooting interests and entertainment choices.

THREE

LABOR PAINS

THE MODERN NFL HAD JUST BEEN FORGED when the issue that would roil it for more than two decades—and which would provide my father with the chance to make his most significant contribution to the league—surfaced. It would also be the biggest strain of his professional life.

The players union that later became known as the National Football League Players Association was not even recognized by the NFL as the official bargaining agent for the players until early 1968. In July, with players dissatisfied with minimum salaries and their pension fund, and talks with owners stalled, players voted 377-17 to strike. Owners countered by declaring a lockout. Players were asking for pension funding of $3 million by 1970. Owners responded that they could not possibly plan ahead to 1970 because of the complexities of the merger. Less than two weeks later, the work stoppage was over. Owners agreed to contribute about $1.5 million to the players' pension fund and establish minimum salaries of $9,000 for rookies, $10,000 for veterans and $50 per preseason game.

The 1970 merger of the leagues also meant there was a merger of the two unions that represented players of the AFL and NFL. Rooney was involved in negotiating the first collective bargaining agreement of the merged league with Ed Garvey, who would soon become the executive director of the newly combined NFL Players Association. My mother remembers that there was a great deal of suspicion about Garvey among owners, because he was perceived as militant in his advocacy of players. My father was, she remembers, one of the few people who could talk to him. An agreement was reached—after a two-day-long strike and a threat by owners to cancel the season—that included increased minimum salaries and improved pension benefits. It was an appropriate bit of foreshadowing of the labor strife to come.

Dan Rooney met Paul Tagliabue during that negotiation. Tagliabue was the NFL's outside counsel then and would become the commissioner in 1989, so this was the beginning of a partnership that wended through strikes, lawsuits, negotiations and, finally, an extended period of labor peace. My father spent so much of his time on labor, and as a result spent so much time with lawyers, including Tagliabue, that he told my brother Art he should become a lawyer. Art did.

Labor deals in professional sports are unique because players are both the labor force and the product. Maintaining labor peace means maintaining the product. Providing the certainty to television networks that the games would continue without disruption has been critical to the league's ability to negotiate ever-more-lucrative television contracts, the lifeblood of the business.

My dad was 24 and barely out of college in 1956 when my grandfather sent him as the Steelers' representative to the first meeting where players were seeking a collective negotiation. The player demands, in hindsight, were amusingly simple: They wanted to be paid for preseason games and be given a second pair of shoes.

At those earlier stages, many of the team owners thought there shouldn't even be a union. My grandfather was the one who put forward a league resolution to recognize the players' union at the fall league meeting of 1956. It passed, but not without significant resistance from Halas and Marshall, who at one point in the meeting shouted, "We can't give in!"

My father and grandfather were outliers among their peers, and it would not be the last time. Their approach toward the players' union was informed by my grandfather's life. He grew up in Coulterville, a Monongahela Valley coal town. It was a union town. His father ran a saloon. His mother was the daughter of a coal miner. Not surprisingly, my grandfather was often more sympathetic to labor than other owners, although he always voted on the side of management.

My father's sympathies had long tilted toward players, too. Because the Steelers were born around the same time as he was, my father grew up like a player. He went to training camp and helped his father at Pitt Stadium and Forbes Field. He made friends with the players. The players nurtured him. He played and loved the game.

Later, in his 20s, when my parents were just married, my father coached the St. Peter's Elementary team. Nobody had much then, but Dan took good care of the kids, making sure they had food. They practiced under a streetlight in the park, and he even had playbooks for the kids. One of his quarterbacks, Mike Hayden, grew up to be a four-star Air Force general, director of the National Security Agency and the Central Intelligence Agency.

My dad's attachment to the game was rooted in his belief that football was a microcosm of life. What the game presented its players on the field mirrored what we are faced with in life: fierce competition and intellectual challenges, and the need to plan and strategize and outwit—not just outhit—opponents. And he believed that work was essential for self-esteem.

As a result, Dan did not look at the players or their union as the enemy but as a group with whom the owners had to figure out a way to work and be partners with. That was his attitude throughout decades of labor strife, a period my brother Art remembers as having a strike or threat of strike every time the collective bargaining agreement expired. Dan Rooney's approach was not always the majority view—many owners wanted to take a harder line against players—but it made him the go-to guy in the league to end or avoid work stoppages.

My father had a philosophy about all types of challenges, which NFL counsel Jeff Pash recalled as: "Sometimes it has to get worse before it can get better."

As a result, he did not panic or get depressed when things went south. He thought it was the thing that would bring everyone back to their senses. He was frustrated by work stoppages—my mother remembers him slamming the door once or twice when he was upset with negotiations. But even when a problem like labor strife was causing him stress, he enjoyed the process of trying to reach a deal. For him, the enjoyment did not come in the finished product. He loved having a vision, and then the journey that would help him construct that vision.

That is why while finding labor peace was one of the greatest accomplishments of his life, he did not pause too long to celebrate it. He was on to the next project in short order.

The owners and players were on a roller coaster of relationships throughout much of the 1970s and 1980s, with nastiness and bitterness ever present. Giants president John Mara, whose father Wellington worked closely with Dan on labor matters, remembers being at training camp in the early 1970s, at a time when the union was talking about going out on strike.

The labor relationship went from bad to worse and got better only briefly before the cycle started over during the most tumultuous, contentious period in league history.

"The owners were not used to having to deal with agents," John Mara recalled. "All of a sudden, it's a new ballgame with Ed Garvey and a players union that was becoming a force to be reckoned with."

Case in point: After the 1970 season was played without a signed labor agreement, the deal, set to expire in 1974, was finally entered into on June 17, 1971. Less than a year later, players sued the league in federal court in Minnesota, challenging what was known as the "Rozelle Rule" as a violation of federal antitrust laws. The rule allowed the NFL commissioner to award compensation, which included players or draft picks, to a team that lost a free agent if both the signing team and the team the player was leaving could not come to an agreement on compensation. The practical effect was that the Rozelle Rule stifled player movement, making what was called free agency at the time virtually meaningless because few teams would be willing to sign free agents if they were at risk of having their rosters raided. Between 1963, when the rule was put in place, and 1974, just four players moved to new teams.

That case—known by the name of the president of the union, the great Colts tight end John Mackey—did not go to trial until 1975, when Tagliabue put Dan Rooney on the stand. But things were hardly quiet before then. The Steelers were a rising power in the early 1970s, making the playoffs in 1972 and again in 1973. But 1974 started inauspiciously. With the lawsuit unresolved and the collective bargaining agreement expired, the players' union, in a move orchestrated by Garvey, went out on strike in July. They declared "No Freedom, No Football" and their cause was the same as the one spelled out in the lawsuit—they wanted to eliminate the Rozelle Rule and the college draft.

The owners were resistant. They feared that true free agency would encourage teams to raid each other's rosters and would upset the competitive balance of the league, which had already been achieved through revenue sharing and the college draft, which gave the worst teams the best picks. The owners labeled what they thought the result would be: "Anarchy."

Mackey once explained in The New York Times how free agency came to be his cause.

"What most people don't know is that my commitment stemmed mostly from one incident in the NFL in which I was handed a piece of paper, a contract, and was told to sign it," Mackey wrote. "Of course I didn't, and from that moment of youthful pique evolved the fight by NFL players to choose for whom they work."

There was little unity among players this time, though. Rookies and free agents had already reported to training camp at Saint Vincent College, a small leafy campus of rolling hills in Latrobe, Pennsylvania. Rooney arrived on the first day of camp and encountered a picket line of some of his veteran players. The quarterback, Terry Bradshaw, and other veterans would not cross the picket line of their teammates, but the rookies and some older players—who feared they would lose their opportunity to play—did report. One of the Steelers' quarterbacks, Joe Gilliam, told Dan Rooney he was about to cross the picket line.

" 'It's my only chance to make this team,' " Dan recalled Gilliam saying. " 'If I don't cross, I know I'm gone. This is my shot.' "

His advice to Gilliam was direct: "You've got to do what you think is right."

The scene was not like those portrayed in movies. My father remembered it as a bunch of players—a few of them with signs, most with mustaches and long hair as was typical of the time—talking and loafing around. There was no hostility. Dan asked the team's player representative, Rocky Bleier, if it was OK if he talked to the players. Bleier said it was OK and stood beside him as they tried to answer the players' questions.

By the time his conversation with the striking players was over, my father had compiled a list of their grievances—it was 93 items long. He told them he respected their right to organize and negotiate. And he said the league would make every effort to work things out.

His fellow owners, though, would not budge and, with little leverage, the players went back to work on August 10—41 days after they walked out. The NFL got a brief reprieve.

Dan Rooney liked the role of potential peacemaker and he found himself repeatedly having to testify in court. Tagliabue and James McKay, a senior partner at the league's law firm, Covington & Burling, were the attorneys charged with preparing Dan for his testimony, which would be given at the trial in Minneapolis.

"When Dan came to Minnesota, there was a tornado warning," Tagliabue remembered. "Jim McKay used to tell the story about how he and Dan had to lock themselves in the bathroom because there was a four-hour storm warning to stay away from the windows. So before Dan testified, Jim McKay sat on the head and Dan sat on the bathtub to prepare his testimony."

The NFL argued that elimination of the Rozelle Rule would lead to the wholesale movement of players because they would make themselves free agents by playing out their contracts. Then, the richest teams could sign the best players, eventually destroying competition. The league pointed to baseball star Catfish Hunter, a pitcher, who had recently become a free agent and signed a five-year contract with the Yankees for $3.75 million.

During sworn testimony, Dan Rooney maintained how important the league believed balance was to their success.

"I think that the fans want to see a contest," Dan said in response to a question during direct examination. "And I think they want to see an evenly matched game and one that, you know, is a struggle."

When he was asked his opinion about what effect the elimination of the Rozelle Rule might have, Dan Rooney attested that if players playing out their option and becoming free agents became rampant, the entire pay structure of the

NFL would change drastically, with the emergence of superstars getting a much bigger share of each team's salary pool.

The court did not agree.

On December 30, 1975, Judge Earl Larson held that the Rozelle Rule was an unreasonable restraint on players' freedom, was anticompetitive and violated antitrust laws.

It was a thunderous defeat for the NFL and it would not be the last one. But it was also the catalyst that pushed the league to restart negotiations toward a new collective bargaining agreement.

"They took those losses hard," John Mara said. "They thought they were building the league up to that point, moving in a great direction, and they viewed the players' efforts as stunting growth and possibly creating competitive imbalance. As is often the case, you think it's the end of the world, and then you learn to adapt to it."

The league created the NFL Management Council to determine labor policy and named six owners to the Council Executive Committee to negotiate directly with the union. Wellington Mara, the chairman of the committee, appointed Dan Rooney as the chief negotiator. It was a nod to Dan's earlier success in negotiations, but it also cast a spotlight on the lack of unity among those key owners. Mara and Rooney were viewed as the voices of reason, Browne said, while others like Dallas' Tex Schramm were hardliners against the union. Dan Rooney liked to be part of developing solutions, and the same sense of responsibility he had as the eldest son to take care of his family permeated his approach to negotiations. He had been with the elders of the NFL from its early years and he felt a sense of ownership of the league. He felt a responsibility to accomplish a mission.

The truth is that even Wellington Mara and Dan Rooney were not early fans of free agency. "He felt early on that it would be the downfall of the NFL," John Mara said of his father. Wellington Mara worried that, especially without a salary cap, certain teams would go crazy signing players and would create competitive imbalance.

That was the foundation of their initial resistance to free agency: that the league was only as strong as its weakest link, and that if the NFL had free agency, irresponsible teams would spend wildly and become dominant. That, they determined, was not in the long-term best interests of the league.

Rooney started talks with the union, which led to a 77-day stay in New York, and meetings in Chicago, Las Vegas and Miami. It was exhausting and often tedious work and it sometimes took a physical toll—his arthritis would always seem to worsen when labor relations were at their lowest points. All to no avail. Tagliabue felt that Ed Garvey and the law firm that had won the antitrust judgment in Minnesota had become impossible to deal with after the league's loss.

That is when Dan Rooney began back-channel negotiations with Dick Anderson, the Miami Dolphins safety and the NFLPA president, who had been elected to his leadership role by the player representatives for all the teams. Such small side conversations are not unusual during labor negotiations. Anderson had sparred with Garvey, because he believed Garvey was too quick to call for player strikes. Those, Anderson thought, were too costly to players, who have short careers and earnings windows.

The negotiation with Rooney, though, had a wrinkle. Anderson wasn't legally authorized to negotiate on behalf of the union. The talks were so secretive that even Garvey, who was supposed to be the lead negotiator for players, did not know about them. Miami Dolphins Coach Don Shula—the same coach who had lost Super Bowl III to the Jets just before the merger went into effect and then crafted the NFL's only undefeated season in Miami in 1972—cooperated with the talks. He allowed Dan to talk to Anderson privately, an unusual situation considering the talks were happening in the middle of the 1976 football season.

The backdrop of the times is worth remembering. St. Louis Cardinals centerfielder Curt Flood had already challenged—and lost at the Supreme Court—baseball's reserve clause. In 1976, pitchers Andy Messersmith and Dave McNally agreed to play without a contract. They were later ruled free agents by an arbitrator. Baseball's reserve clause was crumbling and free agency was in the air.

What Anderson remembers envisioning with Dan Rooney then is remarkable—a free agency system that would have provided movement for players while ensuring that teams would have some type of compensation to provide the opportunity to maintain competitive balance.

The key piece of the deal: Every player in the league would be given a score, with the point system based on things like All-Pro status, starting status, yards gained for running backs, passes caught for receivers, and more position-specific statistics. The players with the bottom 50 percent of scores in the league would become free agents upon the expiration of their contracts. The top 50 percent would become free agents when their contracts expired, too, but the team that signed them would have to give up draft picks to the team losing them. To sign one of the very top players, for instance, the signing team might have to give up two first-round picks.

It was the first glimmer of full free agency.

By then, Dan Rooney had realized that the Rozelle Rule was not coming back. Preserving competitive balance was his priority and he was willing to consider all the mechanisms that could maintain it—salary cap, signing limits, compensatory picks, rights of first refusal and franchise tags.

The Anderson-Rooney agreement, as it came to be known, included the first seeds of many of the things that are standard in the NFL's collective bargaining agreements now. But when Garvey got wind of it, he exploded, furious that he had been excluded from negotiations. The NFLPA would not accept it and Joe Browne, the league's former public relations executive, isn't sure the hard-line owners would have liked it any better.

"They were hard-line because they had no reason not to be," Anderson said recently. "They realized it was going to cost them a lot more money. That was the reason they didn't want it. They didn't have to pay the players. Dan was more progressive than a lot of the owners were. More importantly, he cared about the players themselves. He realized that it was a one-sided deal, that players had no negotiating power."

Dan continued meeting with Anderson after the NFLPA rejected the first deal, and what they came up with became the cornerstone of a new CBA. In 1977, it was ratified—a CBA worth $107 million that allowed for the college draft to continue through 1986, included a no-strike, no-suit clause, instituted a 43-man active player limit, reduced pension vesting to four years, increased minimum salaries and modified player movement and control practices.

The players did not get everything they wanted—there was still not full free agency—but it was still more than they started with. And Dan and other owners had recognized that labor peace and not total victory was the crucial component of a deal, so that both sides could feel as if they had walked away having made a gain.

Those negotiations also included another crucial win. My father had met and gotten to know Gene Upshaw, the Raiders' premier offensive lineman who was a player representative. Their relationship—which would grow so close that Upshaw would spend nights in my parents' home during future negotiations— was critical to solving the increasingly contentious and damaging labor battles to come.

When that agreement expired in 1982, the NFLPA called for another strike. This one was a doozy. After the first two games of the regular season were played, the players walked out. And stayed out, for 57 days. Eight weeks of games were canceled, making the strike the most extensive work stoppage in NFL history.

It had already been a bruising year for the league. Back in May, a jury had ruled in favor of the Oakland Raiders and Al Davis, deciding that the NFL had violated federal antitrust rules by refusing to allow the Raiders to move to the Los Angeles Coliseum. The Raiders moved south—the already tense relationship between most of the NFL and Davis got even more fraught— and the entire season was in limbo.

The first suggestion that something had to give came in mid-November when the television networks announced that they had lost viewers in record numbers. The drop-dead date to salvage any semblance of a season was Thanksgiving Day, November 25.

There were long days and nights of negotiating and at one point Dan was ready to quit. "We are not giving another dollar," he told negotiators as the meeting broke up and he headed to his hotel.

Around midnight, Paul Martha, a labor arbitrator who had played running back for the Steelers in the 1960s, called my father's hotel room.

Rooney told Martha he was heading home in the morning, but Martha implored him to stay. The next day, the logjam broke and a deal was made.

It was another bandage on the problem that had yet to be fully solved. The deal ran through 1986. There was a minimum salary schedule based on seniority, training camp and postseason pay was increased, benefits were improved and a severance pay system was introduced. But the veteran free agent system was left unchanged.

Still, trust was building between my father and Upshaw, in particular, and that would become important in the coming years.

The owners had learned something important during that strike, though. Many veteran players would have crossed the picket line if there had been a viable alternative to striking. With the expiration of that deal looming in 1987, owners anticipated a strike—and they were ready.

Tex Schramm and Hugh Culverhouse pushed for teams to recruit replacement players in anticipation of another strike. Dan sensed that they had no real interest in making a deal with the players. They wanted to break them and proceed with a season played with, as he wrote in his own book, "retired pros, collegiate has-beens and NFL wannabes."

Upshaw had taken over as the executive director of the NFLPA shortly after the 1982 deal was completed. Pash believes Culverhouse, Schramm and some other hard-liners were testing Upshaw in his first go-around as the union's chief.

At the start of the 1987 negotiations, at a meeting in Philadelphia between the league's executive committee and player representatives just before the start of the season, Upshaw made one final pitch for some form of free agency.

Schramm was obstinate and uttered the incendiary words that have hung over the relationship between players and team owners ever since.

Upshaw relayed his account of what happened to the sportswriter Bob St. John, author of a biography of Schramm, when he raised the question of free agency.

"Tex Schramm screamed at me across the bargaining table, 'You're not going to get it! You're not going to get it in five years, you're not going to get it in 10 years, and you're not going to ever see it.'"

"'Don't you see?'" Schramm concluded. "'You're the cattle. We're the ranchers.'"

Whatever bond there was between labor and management was shattered. The NFL canceled the games of week 3 and teams—including the Steelers—scrambled to sign replacement players.

In Pittsburgh, Dan Rooney worried that our replacement players would be harassed. So the team moved its base of operations about 60 miles away, to Johnstown, with negotiations with replacement players taking place in a Holiday Inn hotel room. Across the league, the replacement players were mostly leftovers from the failed United States Football League and the folded Montreal Alouettes of the Canadian Football League, as well as players who had been cut in the preseason or who had washed out of the NFL in previous years. There were bartenders and firefighters. The plan was for the teams to play their regularly scheduled games with the replacements.

Because of the structure of the league at the time, Rozelle played little role in labor negotiations, with the management council handling it on behalf of owners and Rozelle, at least theoretically, remaining neutral. As a result, from 1983 to 1989—when, with Dan Rooney's help, Tagliabue became the commissioner and wrested control of labor for his office—it was unclear who was in charge of labor relations on the league side, and that certainly did not smooth the path of negotiations. Even the small group of owners who were most involved were split. And Rozelle agreed with the moderates. He thought the use of replacement players was a huge mistake, an affront to the networks, their viewers and their advertisers. He feared using replacement players risked destroying the credibility of the league with fans and players. The union assumed that even if replacement teams were cobbled together, television stations would not air substandard football.

The owners called the players' bluff. With more veteran players crossing the picket line than expected—including such big names as Joe Montana—and the games drawing modest crowds and television audiences, the players had no leverage. The games were a stain on the NFL, but the owners had won a short-term tactical victory. And they wanted to make sure the players knew it.

"I remember in '87 when Jack Donlan, executive director of the Management Council, was in Pete's office and players were coming across, so we knew it wasn't going to last much longer," said Joe Browne. "Donlan was on the phone with Upshaw and Pete was sitting there. Gene said, 'We'll come back this week.' Donlan said, 'No, no, no. You can't come back this week. You've got to sit out one more week and then come back.' Pete later said he almost became physically ill after Donlan took such a hard-line approach. He was trying to put a foot on their neck and teach them a lesson and that made Pete sick."

After players voted to end their strike, they took their fight to court, filing another antitrust suit in Minnesota federal court. This case challenged the right of first refusal in the compensation system.

This was a particularly difficult time for my father. After the replacement games, Rozelle turned to Dan Rooney and Jim Finks, along with Tagliabue, to work with the union representatives to try to come up with a new system, without the input of the management council. That infuriated Hugh Culverhouse, owner of the Tampa Bay Buccaneers, who was the new chair of the management committee. Dan thought self-made businessmen who then bought NFL teams had a significant blind spot: They thought hardball tactics that worked in other businesses translated to football. Dan Rooney kept telling Culverhouse the hard-line approach was a huge mistake.

"This is a different business than other businesses," he would say. "You can't have these guys hating us."

Culverhouse was so furious that he demanded Dan Rooney be thrown out of the league. My father would go into meetings and laugh at Culverhouse.

Rooney was essentially ostracized by the rest of the management council. Tagliabue was, too, when they realized he was working with Rooney and Finks. Dan

Rooney had come the closest during the replacement games with Upshaw to having an agreement that would have resolved the problem.

The hard-line owners felt they had achieved a clear win over the players.

But my father had a much longer view.

"We're not going to have a deal without free agency," he predicted. He always put the emphasis on the word "free." Pash remembers that Dan Rooney felt that, ultimately, the league would have to come up with a deal that gave every player a real opportunity to become a free agent at some point in his career. That didn't mean he would definitely be a free agent, or that he would reach free agency at the best time in his career. But the opportunity would exist.

There was a lot of initial resistance to that idea from some owners, but Dan Rooney and other moderates kept pressing the point. Other owners, especially the ones who were not involved in negotiations, were watching the court cases and could envision their nightmare scenario. The court could go against them, giving all players unrestricted free agency and putting owners on the hook for hundreds of millions in damages.

And they began to realize that ongoing talks were going nowhere, that between the time the strike ended in 1987 and 1989—when there was still no new collective bargaining agreement—Culverhouse wasn't trying to get a deal done. Instead, he wanted to crush Upshaw and the union and he was confident he could outlast Rozelle.

The year 1989 was one of seismic change for the NFL, and they were changes that led to the labor system we have today.

With caustic negotiations going nowhere and no new deal in sight, owners unilaterally imposed a system called "Plan B"—as in, "Let's try Plan B."

The system allowed each team to protect 37 of its players (the rosters were 47 men) each year from becoming free agents, leaving the rest free to sign with other teams. A protected player whose contract had expired was theoretically also free to accept an offer from another team. But the team that protected the player could match the offer and retain his services. And if a player's former team chose not to match the contract offer, the new team had to provide compensation to the old team in the form of draft choices.

Plan B led to more player movement, but not by the best players—who, of course, were the ones protected. The New York Times reported that just two protected players changed teams under Plan B.

And in March, Rozelle announced his retirement after 29 years in charge, worn out from the constant labor and legal battles. He told reporters at the league's annual meeting in Palm Desert that he didn't want to die in office like Bert Bell had. And he realized, now that he was in his 60s, that even if he had stayed on until his contract ended after the 1991 season, he wasn't going to be able to fix everything. Owners were hopelessly divided, the labor impasse had no apparent quick end, and there were more court appearances to come.

Rozelle and Dan had grown exceptionally close since they had started collaborating as young men, and they spoke often. Rozelle and his wife, Carrie, would dine regularly with my parents and they took a few trips to Ireland together. Carrie Rozelle and my mother would alternate visits to the boarding school where their children were studying, taking both families' children out to dinner and making sure they were making their grades.

Rozelle had one final assignment for my father: Help make Tagliabue the next commissioner.

Dan had been impressed with Tagliabue in the almost 20 years they had already been working together on labor matters. And in Rozelle's final years as commissioner, Rooney had come to believe that the commissioner had to be fully involved in labor negotiations, that the days of being a neutral observer were over. Tagliabue and my father shared several qualities: They were both former athletes themselves and so had a respect for players, and they were both committed to equality and fairness, in the NFL and in society. They, essentially, had the same worldview. Rooney told Upshaw that Tagliabue could be trusted.

Tagliabue and Upshaw had most recently worked on labor negotiations together. Tagliabue had even cross-examined Upshaw in 1981 during the trial after the

Raiders alleged antitrust violations by the NFL for trying to block the Raiders' move to Los Angeles. Upshaw was a witness for Al Davis, who was arguing how important it was to play in a good stadium, with luxury boxes, which Oakland did not have.

Upshaw, though, was undoubtedly rooting for Tagliabue to become commissioner over Finks, who was viewed as more aligned with the old guard of hardline owners on the management council. Ultimately, the strong relationships among Tagliabue, Upshaw and Rooney were critical to getting labor peace. For years, it remained shocking that Upshaw was so trusted—there were moments when outsiders would stop and think, "But he's a Raider!"

Tagliabue, Upshaw and my father were a really good match, though. Tagliabue was book smart, much more so than Rooney or Upshaw. Dan Rooney carried the heritage of the league and also could envision the possibilities. And Upshaw simply got it. It is selling him short to say he had street smarts. He certainly had that, but he had more. He fought like hell for the players, but he also understood the business of the league and how the pieces fit together. And the three genuinely liked and respected each other.

After Tagliabue got the job, he invited Upshaw out to dinner. He made a conscious decision not to invite Upshaw to one of the prominent Pennsylvania Avenue restaurants frequented by Washington's power brokers, Browne remembers. He took Upshaw to a local restaurant in one of the district's more diverse neighborhoods. Tagliabue did it on purpose, so Upshaw wouldn't be the only African-American in the whole place. Tagliabue wanted Upshaw to feel comfortable, and their relationship grew so strong that it drew criticism from some members of both of their constituencies—a typical indication that a negotiation is not one-sided. Some owners thought Tagliabue gave up too much to the union. Some players thought Upshaw allowed Tagliabue to win too often.

Dan Rooney had already known Upshaw through previous negotiations and they spent long days together during this tumultuous period, trying to hammer out an agreement to bring to a close what seemed to be unending strife. The union had decertified and more litigation was in the works, a challenge to Plan B free agency.

THREE | LABOR PAINS

At one point, Upshaw and my father negotiated for three days straight in the breakfast room of my family's home in the Mt. Lebanon suburb of Pittsburgh. Upshaw slept over two nights in a row, this man who was 10 times the size of Dan, who had played for the team the Steelers loathed, eating eggs my mom had cooked for them.

They were exceptionally collegial; there was no yelling. But there were also moments when neither would budge. They were tough with each other, and they would sit there shaking their heads and laughing. "That is never going to happen" was uttered more than once. They both knew how to negotiate in tiny increments, sometimes to no avail. But at least the conversation kept going.

Upshaw died in August 2008, just three days after being diagnosed with pancreatic cancer. Pash remembers Tagliabue saying that Upshaw was a great person to have on the other side of a negotiating table because Upshaw was both an offensive lineman and a Raider. That meant he understood the importance of structure and of having a game plan. He appreciated the need for people to work together, because no unit in football requires more coordination and communication than the offensive line. And because he had worked for Al Davis, Upshaw could respect strong ownership and leadership.

That didn't mean the owners could get everything they wanted. But at least they were dealing with someone with whom they felt they could have a conversation.

Those conversations and the established relationship took on added weight when the challenge to Plan B free agency was at full throttle, with the trial that began in 1992 in a federal courthouse in Minneapolis. The players' union handed out to media members copies of all the financial statements of every team. USA Today published significant private information, including personal salaries. At least one executive's ex-wife reopened her alimony case as a result. Needless to say, management was furious.

Meanwhile, Upshaw, Tagliabue and Rooney were still talking, trying to get a deal done before the jury returned a verdict on whether Plan B violated antitrust laws. The release of the financial information put a lot of pressure on everyone. Players and owners were still tangling over free agency, in this case how many years a player would have to be in the league before becoming a free agent. Owners wanted some players to be exempt—the birth of franchise players—but the union balked at how many would be exempt and what the compensation to a team would be if another team signed those players. The sides were achingly close to a deal but could not get it done.

So the court forced them to finish.

After 16 hours of deliberation, the eight-woman jury ruled that Plan B was too restrictive and violated antitrust law. But the jury struck a delicate balance. While the union's lawyers declared victory, the jury awarded no damages to four of the eight plaintiffs, and relatively paltry damages to the others.

"It was basically a message to both sides," Jeff Pash concluded. " 'NFL, you're not going to be able to continue with this kind of approach. Players, if you think there's a big jackpot here, forget it, because it ain't happening.' "

The union quickly filed a new lawsuit designed to get a handful of players who had not yet signed for the 1992 season declared free agents immediately. Judge David Doty, the district judge in Minnesota who came to play an outsized role in NFL labor history—often at the league's expense—granted an injunction giving those players free agency.

There was a meeting in Doty's chambers, with Upshaw and the union's lawyers and Wellington Mara, Al Davis, Paul Tagliabue and Dan.

Browne, who was also in the room, remembers Doty saying that he had his decision ready and if the two sides could not reach an agreement, he would issue it. With a warning: "Commissioner Tagliabue, you're not going to like it and neither are you, Mr. Upshaw."

Doty then met with both sides separately. They had been close before the verdict, but they needed the push over the top. First, Doty met with Upshaw. Then Doty went to the league's group, essentially acting as a mediator.

Browne remembers Doty telling the owners that if they couldn't reach an agreement, they would have a two-round draft, free agency after three years and a few other things.

Davis said, "Your honor, if all those things are in there, what's in there that Upshaw doesn't like?"

Everyone in the room laughed, but Doty's threat was enough. The sides met again and finally came up with the system that it has today: free agency, with a draft, franchise tags and a salary cap. My father was a big proponent of a hard cap as the most crucial mechanism to maintaining competitive balance. Tagliabue was initially not as big a believer in it, but he realized it was a more palatable position than the anti-free agency stand other owners took. Upshaw knew the salary cap would be a hard sell, but he believed the players' biggest concern was getting true free agency and some percentage of gross revenue.

After decisions to share revenue equally and to merge with the AFL, this was the third historic decision that led to the modern NFL.

Many years later, Upshaw said about the episode in Doty's chambers, "I wonder if he had anything in that damn envelope."

It took years, long after he was involved in labor relations, for Wellington Mara to agree that the advent of free agency had been good for the league.

"You find out," his son John said, "it's not the end of the world."

The extended run of labor peace that the league enjoyed after those disputes ended seemed to prove Dan Rooney's theory that the long-term impact of having peace was more important than winning on every detail. Fans, television networks and sponsors knew there would be no more canceled games. It was worth investing again, financially and emotionally, in the future of the NFL. The bottom line bears that out. Total league revenue between 1952 and 1956 averaged $10.4 million. In 2018, it was roughly $15 billion. The stability offered by labor peace was a bedrock of that growth.

FOUR

GROWTH AND DISLOCATION

AS CAUSTIC AS THE NFL'S LABOR FIGHTS WERE, there were few issues more personally wrenching for my father than team relocation. One in particular, the 1995 move of the Cleveland Browns to Baltimore, caused a fissure in one of his closest friendships that never fully healed.

Revenue from stadiums is the second-greatest source of money in the NFL, behind only the mammoth television contracts. Beginning in the early 1960s and continuing for several decades, NFL teams often played in publicly financed stadiums that were primarily used by baseball teams, like Pittsburgh's Three Rivers Stadium, which the Steelers shared with the Pirates. There wasn't much to recommend those stadiums. Because they were being built around the same time as Americans were leaving cities to move to the suburbs, they were often constructed near highways and the oval buildings were surrounded by vast parking lots. They were sterile and had little charm—one of their nicknames was "concrete doughnuts"—and when the baseball and football seasons overlapped, the infield dirt cut a swath through the gridiron.

Their major selling point was their price—for the teams, it was minimal because the public footed most of the bill.

Very few new stadiums were built only for NFL teams through the 1980s. As NFL revenue exploded in the early 1990s, it became obvious that it would be increasingly difficult to get public funds to finance the construction of new stadiums. If teams wanted a new building, they would have to find ways to privately finance significant portions of the ballooning costs.

As a result, in the mid-1990s, the NFL was facing a run of franchise instability. With the advent of free agency, teams needed more cash on hand to pay signing bonuses and the like. That means they needed to generate revenue they would not have to share with the other teams. Stadium revenue—from suite sales, for instance—is not shared among teams. So teams that needed revenue went looking for new stadiums and they found them in smaller markets that were willing to foot the bill to build those stadiums while bigger markets were not. The Rams and Raiders had left Los Angeles—the country's second-largest television market—to go to St. Louis and Oakland (a return engagement for the Raiders), respectively. The Houston Oilers announced that they would relocate to Nashville. The Patriots flirted with leaving the Boston suburb of Foxborough to move to Hartford, Conn.

During the early weeks of the 1995 season, after spending years negotiating attempted enhancements to Cleveland Municipal Stadium, Art Modell called Dan with bad news.

My family's connection to Cleveland stretched back to visits in the 1940s. Pittsburgh and Cleveland are strikingly similar. Separated by just a two-hour drive, they had foundations in steel and manufacturing. As a young man, my father hung out in bars in the Flats and at Terminal Tower. As he got older, he ate in the restaurants of Little Italy and spent spring and summer nights at friends' homes on the Chagrin River. Later, three of his nine children attended school in Cleveland. As a licensed pilot, Rooney made the 28-minute flight from Pittsburgh to Cuyahoga County and Burke Lakefront airports routinely.

Paul Brown, the legendary coach, founded the team that bore his name in 1945 and won the championship of the All-American Football Conference in the Browns' first five years of existence. When the conference folded, the Browns joined the NFL in 1950 and proceeded to win the championship in their first year in the league. In all, they went to the championship game of their league every one of the first 10 years of the team's existence.

And that was good for the Steelers.

When the Steelers needed financial help to survive in the late 1940s and 1950s, the Browns' entrance into the NFL made the difference. The Steelers received 40 percent of the sold-out gate receipts in Cleveland and 60 percent of the gate when throngs of Browns fans traveled to Pittsburgh for Steelers home games.

The link to Cleveland grew even stronger when Modell bought the team in 1961. While my father focused his attention on labor, Modell, a former television producer and advertising man, emerged as one of the league's primary leaders on television. Their work went hand in hand for decades as the league grew, and their families became personally close.

But when Modell called Dan Rooney in 1995, he told him that he planned to leave Cleveland and move his team to Baltimore. Dan was stunned and upset because he did not believe team movement was good for the league and because he had considered Modell to be like him, a league man who would put the interests of the NFL over his own. He implored Modell to stay, telling him that Browns fans, like Steelers fans, were the most loyal in the game.

When it became clear that Modell would not turn back, Dan Rooney told him: "I'm for Cleveland."

This was an emotional experience for my father. He thought leaving Cleveland—like Pittsburgh, a place where football was invented—and its fans was both immoral and impractical. It was simply wrong. And he thought the NFL could not keep saying it was the good guys and then keep doing bad things.

My father would have preferred that his friendship with Modell not be strained, but he believed Modell had crossed a line. Modell was hurt that Dan had chosen loyalty to the league over loyalty to their personal friendship, and he was angry that Dan quickly became one of the prime people pushing to put a team back in Cleveland. In his later years, my father looked like a cuddly old man. But that countenance belied his love of a good argument and his iron will.

It was, certainly, the most brutal test of Dan's determination not to bend his values, which emphasized what was best for the league. And he did not let a personal relationship get in the way of that.

Still, my mother knows my father was pained by the fissure with Modell. They had been close for more than 30 years, and she has often said that a little bit of their friendship died with the move. My mother remembers it took several years before Modell and my father would even acknowledge each other when they were in the same hallway at league meetings or at games. The strain even extended to my mother's friendship with Modell's wife, Patti.

In the late 1990s, the Steelers would go through a similar, sometimes dispiriting, struggle to get a new stadium built in Pittsburgh. Roger Goodell was an executive for the league under Tagliabue and he remembers a phone call with Rooney and Tagliabue after a vote on stadium funding had gone against the Steelers. The conversation was essentially about whether Dan should threaten to move the Steelers out of Pittsburgh if public money was not made available for a stadium.

"He was very opposed to it," Goodell said. "He never wanted to do that. He said, 'I know, I've seen it, I saw what others have done. I don't wanna do it that way.'"

Goodell thinks Modell's experience went through his head as the Steelers struggled for a stadium, and he knew he could not even threaten to move after being so critical of Modell's decision. And he believes Dan felt Modell overreacted when the Cleveland Indians got a new baseball stadium and he was still facing headwinds.

In a Saturday meeting with Cleveland officials in New York just before Modell made his announcement, Goodell and Tagliabue quickly worked out an arrangement to keep the Browns' name, colors and team records and archives with the city of Cleveland, essentially putting the Browns franchise in a state of suspended animation. Modell could take his players to Baltimore, but it would function almost as an expansion team. Any remnants of his old franchise had to stay back in Cleveland, in anticipation of a team eventually being there again.

Then began the painstaking process of securing a commitment for a new stadium that would be largely paid for by the league and deciding whether the team for Cleveland would be an expansion team or a relocation. Goodell recalls that Dan was instrumental in convincing the mayor of Cleveland that he had to take the lead in getting the new stadium built.

Over the course of three years, the job of returning a team to Cleveland—from getting the stadium built to deciding to make it an expansion team to finding the right owners—fell largely to Goodell and Dan Rooney. Tagliabue, who knew his friend Dan Rooney could take it, was well aware that Modell did not want a team to be put in Cleveland. The commissioner wanted to distance himself from the fray. Tagliabue would cast Goodell and Rooney as the bad guys to keep the peace with Modell.

Dan Rooney had known Goodell before the Cleveland project, but they grew exceptionally close during that period.

Goodell said my father taught him how to think about league issues and how to get things done. They worked together on some of the most difficult issues the league faced: Cleveland, realignment, the Rooney Rule. There was nothing they did not talk about. Dan Rooney was mentoring Goodell and preparing him to be the commissioner, although he never told Goodell that directly.

In 1999, the Browns, then owned by the Lerner family—Al Lerner, ironically, had helped his friend Modell move the team to Baltimore—resumed play in a new stadium in Cleveland. And the Baltimore Ravens took the place of the Browns as the Steelers' most heated rival. And when the Ravens beat the Giants in Super Bowl XXXV, five years after they left Cleveland, Dan went into the Ravens locker room and embraced his old friend Modell.

The entire experience, though, convinced Tagliabue and Dan Rooney that the NFL had two systemic problems on its hands: One was the skyrocketing cost of stadiums, and the increasing difficulty of getting the public to pay for them; the other was the need to keep teams from relocating, particularly from large television markets to smaller ones.

My father's opposition to relocation was rooted in his dual priorities: the well-being of the fans and the league.

He thought the rupturing of relationships with fans that resulted from relocation was potentially ruinous, particularly when teams left areas with large numbers and multiple generations of fans. It was, too, bad business for teams to abandon larger television markets for smaller ones. The move of the Rams from Los Angeles to St. Louis, for example, was a negative in television terms.

The NFL had just signed a round of big television contracts when Senator Arlen Specter of Pennsylvania introduced a bill in the summer of 1999 to require the NFL and Major League Baseball to put 10 percent of their network television revenues each year into a fund. The leagues would have to use that money to pay at least half the costs of all new stadiums. Teams would pay 25 percent and local governments would chip in the remaining 25 percent. Specter used words like "blackmail," "extortion" and "thievery" to describe attempts by the leagues to get the public to pay for stadiums.

Specter's bill went nowhere, but it got plenty of attention. And grudgingly, some owners came around to thinking that the idea supported by Tagliabue had some merit. If the NFL was going to try to convince cities and states that a single-purpose football stadium that would be used far fewer days each year than a baseball stadium or a basketball arena was something they should support, the NFL would have to make it attractive for them.

Dan Rooney suggested the NFL should approach this issue in much the same way it had approached revenue sharing—that the entire league would benefit if every team had a first-class stadium for its fans and players. At a dinner meeting with Tagliabue and a few others, he proposed having every team contribute a portion of its television money to a fund that would support stadium construction.

In a way, this was the television revenue sharing model in reverse. With the television money, the biggest markets sacrificed what would have been greater television revenue to keep the smaller markets competitive. With stadium construction, the smaller markets were contributing to a pool that would ultimately benefit larger market clubs by helping them build stadiums.

That, of course, upset some owners. They felt it was a subsidy for big market clubs, and that the program would disproportionately help the wealthier teams in the larger markets. Dan agreed that was true. Some teams might benefit more than others in the short term. But in the long term, the entire league would benefit from keeping teams in the largest markets.

Other owners were concerned that the league funds would simply replace public money and that stadiums would remain difficult to finance without public support. Rooney argued the opposite was more likely, that the willingness of the league to use a portion of its ballooning revenue would, in fact, encourage state and local governments to contribute, too. It would make it clear to cities and states that the entire NFL stood behind a building project.

Most important, my father believed the NFL investment in new stadiums would be shared by players, who would not only benefit from improved workplace conditions and more stable relationships with their community, but who also would get a share of the increased revenue new stadiums would generate.

With labor peace finally in hand, Tagliabue and Rooney worked with Upshaw and the players' union on a complex agreement. The union would give credits against the salary cap for stadium investment. The players would be partners in the private component of stadium financing. A team that wanted a new stadium would receive a loan of up to $150 million from the fund. The loan would be paid back by giving a percentage of club seat revenues from the new stadium. It was a compromise that other owners could embrace.

Almost immediately, the NFL began funding projects. The Patriots, Broncos and Eagles all got funding. So did the Giants and Jets, who got a combined $300 million when they built the shared MetLife Stadium. Most recently, the Minnesota Vikings received $200 million toward the $1.13 billion price tag of U.S. Bank Stadium. The stadium opened in 2016 and the franchise's valuation jumped from $1.59 billion to $2.2 billion, according to the Northwestern Business Review.

Those booming revenues and skyrocketing valuations tell the story of the NFL's growing footprint in American culture. And for Dan Rooney's part in laying the foundation of what the league is now, he enjoyed tremendous respect from his fellow owners. Falcons owner Arthur Blank tells a story about the time when my father, as the chairman of the compensation committee, stood up to announce that Tagliabue's contract had been extended. He offered no details—not how long the contract would run, not the amount of the compensation, or anything about what the negotiation was like. He told the other owners that if they had any questions, they could call him. Blank jokes now that this was hardly a best practice for corporate America. But the other owners showed so much deference to Dan Rooney's judgment that they asked him nothing.

Still, the league he helped build ultimately made my father uneasy. The NFL, the money, the spectacle had all gotten far bigger than my father had ever imagined they would. And, just as he had been initially, he was concerned about what the pursuit of more money would do to the league. He pushed back sometimes, privately and publicly.

Early in the 2000s, some owners were encouraging the league to find ways to mine ever more revenue, to market itself even more aggressively. Sponsor-creep had begun—names of advertisers appeared on jersey decals in NFL Europe, for instance, and every space in the new stadiums was ripe for signage. Goodell was the league's executive vice president, and while he had worked on some of the league's thorniest issues, he was also thought of highly by a segment of owners because he was comfortable with the NFL as an aggressive business.

Dan Rooney often disagreed with Goodell on the avenues the league took in pursuit of more revenue and he warned him of the perils of the path. During one ongoing conversation about league branding, a football jersey arrived at the league office addressed to Goodell. It was made to resemble a NASCAR driver's uniform, adorned with sponsorship decals and corporate logos. Dan had sent the garish jersey to convey a message.

"Our business is the game; we're not in this thing to make all the money in the world," Dan told The New York Times in February 2006 about that jersey. "I think some other teams still do things our way. But on this, we might be the last guy on the mountain."

Dan Rooney resisted the corporatization of football. One league initiative had signs wrapped around the goal posts that read "Feel the Power." Dan took one look at them on the goal posts at Heinz Field and ordered them taken down. Told that the league said they had to be up, my father replied, "We're not feeling the power." And they stayed down.

His most assertive public statement, though, came when, while serving as U.S. ambassador to Ireland, he returned to Pittsburgh in January 2011 for a playoff game. The league would lock out players two months later, but the sides were still negotiating to try to reach a new collective bargaining agreement before the old one expired. The Ambassador was not involved in the negotiations and that might have been just as well. He was frustrated by the lack of progress. Management was pushing for an 18-game regular season, arguing that the extra revenue it would generate from television contracts would facilitate a deal.

My father agreed with other owners, who thought the proceeds of the business were not being fairly shared, and that significant action needed to be taken to adjust the revenue split between teams and players. But he had long opposed the idea of a longer season. He thought it was too much for the players to endure and maybe too greedy for the league. That day, he spoke to three reporters who regularly covered the league.

"I would rather not get the money" than expand the season, Dan said. "You have a system that works. Why add them?"

He understood the power of mass media. And he felt a responsibility to say that the train needed to be slowed down.

He had helped build something and it had grown much bigger than he had ever imagined. Whenever we would leave a game, the last thing my father would say was, "Pull the center pole."

He always felt the spectacle of NFL games was no better than the circus. And that we should all never forget that.

Dan Rooney | Courtesy of Pittsburgh Steelers

Dan Rooney (Art's Son), Art Rooney II, Dan Rooney, Roger Goodell | Courtesy of Pittsburgh Steelers

Paul Tagliabue and Gene Upshaw | Charles Dharapak/Associated Press

Wellington Mara, Patrick Bowlen, Art Modell, Dan Rooney | Al Messerschmidt/Associated Press

Art Rooney Sr. | Rooney Family

Dan Rooney, George Allen, Pete Rozelle | Sam Myers/Associated Press

Mr. & Mrs. Daniel Rooney | Rooney Family

Paul Tagliabue, Chan Tagliabue, Patricia Rooney, Dan Rooney | Al Messerschmidt/Associated Press

Dan Rooney and Art Modell | Courtesy of Pittsburgh Steelers

CONCLUSION

Getting opposing sides to give up something for a greater good, envisioning and articulating long-term goals when others are focused on short-term gains—these were hallmarks of my father's management style. And they were critical when the NFL reached its tipping point in the early 1960s. Persuading owners to agree on sharing the revenue from television was both revolutionary and stabilizing, and led to the birth of the modern NFL.

The first deal the league signed with CBS in 1961, based heavily on the persuasion of my father and grandfather, would lead to a partnership between football and television that continues as the most important underpinning of the NFL's business model to this day. As previously noted, the league signed nine-year deals from 2014 to 2022 with CBS, NBC, Fox and ESPN for a combined total of $39.6 billion—with that revenue split among the league's 32 teams (up from 13 in 1960). The Super Bowl regularly attracts more than 100 million viewers, more than double the average viewership of the World Series.

The bet on the long game the NFL made in the early 1960s has paid off far beyond what those early dealmakers imagined. My father had been one of the central driving forces in creating the foundations of this approach. He took great pride in the industriousness and ingenuity of the endeavor. He enjoyed the league's popularity and the nation's love for the professional game that his father, George Halas, Tim Mara and Charley Bidwill had started. He also, however, always experienced a paradox, an internal fear and angst that warned him against the effort to chase all this money.

STORY II | ARCHITECT:

THE STEELERS
OF THE 1970S

STORY II | ARCHITECT: **THE STEELERS OF THE 1970s**

Night was falling on the Rose Bowl on January 20, 1980, the site of Super Bowl XIV. The Southern California sky was purple, red and orange as the sun set over the San Gabriel Mountains. Although some of the 103,985 fans there were surely rooting for the hometown Los Angeles Rams, the stars of Hollywood that day were the Pittsburgh Steelers.

The Steelers wore their traditional black jerseys with white numbers, and over the previous decade the uniform had become symbolic. The integration of the team during the 1970s had been purposeful, a keystone of my father's leadership of the Steelers. Joe Greene, who went to a segregated high school in Texas, anchored the front of the Steel Curtain defense. Buttressing Greene were future Hall of Famers Jack Lambert and Jack Ham, two white linebackers from the Rust Belt. Behind them were Mel Blount and Donnie Shell, both of whom had attended historically black colleges and universities (HBCUs) and marched in the South after Martin Luther King Jr.'s assassination. The final line of defense was Mike Wagner, a white safety from a town situated between Milwaukee and Chicago.

The ongoing collapse of the steel and manufacturing industries in western Pennsylvania was pushing many Steelers fans into financial ruin. Race relations would be strained by the economic devastation. On that day, though, the Steelers won their fourth Super Bowl. A group of men from vastly different backgrounds had come together to become the greatest football team ever.

That is as my father had intended it. When I consider his role in the making of the Steelers of the 1970s, I think of his vision and design for the entire organization, the management style he deployed and the executive team he hired and with which he worked closely.

My father developed his vision by observing other organizations and other leaders. He was, fortunately, surrounded by successful people and their businesses. He grew up around winning local teams, like baseball's Pirates and the University of Pittsburgh football program. He played on a good football team at North Catholic High

School. He saw how the Giants, Bears, Packers and Browns flourished. His mentors were some of the most successful coaches and executives of their day: Jock Sutherland, George Halas, Vince Lombardi, Bert Bell.

My father took notes, trying to glean lessons from every one of his conversations with those men. He drew images in his notebooks, illustrating what they told him. He was impressed with how Halas, "Papa Bear" of Chicago, commanded the room at meetings of NFL owners. He paid close attention to how Halas tried to drive the league in the direction he thought was best for it. My father would later incorporate that concept—looking out for the greater interest of the league—into his own approach. Bell, a coach, owner and commissioner, often played the role of arbiter as league business was discussed. My father would take on that role, too, and became the consensus builder at some of the most significant moments in Steelers and NFL history.

Those influences shaped his ideas for the Steelers. He expected the Steelers to be great. They would win—and win championships—but he wanted the Steelers to be great in all things. In the community. In their engagement with the outside world. In their thinking. He wanted people who worked for the Steelers to think broadly, to read and learn about things that were uncommon and done well, and then to bring greatness to every effort in their daily lives and work.

Then he wrote very specifically what he expected each person within the organization to do. This plan was his design for the entirety of the franchise. The document was always in the credenza behind his desk and he would refer to it often. It described in detail every activity for which the franchise was responsible. He wrote out the obligations and objectives of each role, from ball boy to business managers to coaches.

The plan guided him and everyone else at the Steelers, but it was not limited to roles and processes. It included a sense of purpose. My father believed the team should be doing something that was meaningful for football and also for Pittsburgh. He wanted people who came to games to feel it was an enriching experience, and when people thought about the Steelers, he wanted them to have the sense that the Steelers were about more than wins and losses. He wanted staff members who would embrace that ethos, and he thought the organization would be stronger if its employees applied their own creativity to reach that goal.

My father's intention to prioritize integration was the most obvious manifestation of his sense of purpose for the team. It was a core element of his plan, and he would labor with his management team to make it come to fruition.

As lofty as his ideals were, my father was a tough and demanding executive. He fired Buddy Parker, one of only two winning coaches in the Steelers' first 40 years. He removed his brother Art Jr. from his job as head of player personnel and also fired Tom Donahoe, another personnel executive who was the grandson of the man who presented my grandfather at his Hall of Fame induction—because he thought both were interfering with the head coach's ability to run the team. He demanded the firing of one of Chuck Noll's assistants, the rare occasion when my father involved himself in a coaching decision. His management style was unequivocal and somewhat unforgiving on one issue: If he thought someone was not contributing to what he felt was the best interest of the organization, he would remove that person.

The closest analogy to how my father led is that of an orchestra conductor. He wanted every piece to be working in concert, to be pulling in the same direction. He did not operate by mandate. He did not issue directives—he wasn't telling anybody specifically which notes of their instrument to play.

Rather, he modeled what he wanted. He was in charge and everything flowed from him, but rather than order that things be done, he influenced his executives with his thoughts, and they in turn bought into his vision and contributed to his accomplishment. Leadership is not all business plans and directives. There is an element of cult of personality to successful leadership, too, and that was a piece of how the Steelers' executive team was inspired by how my father worked.

There was no missing his devotion. He was all-in—heart, soul, mind. Everything about him was focused on making the Steelers great. He was that way with the NFL and Ireland, too, and that focus and enthusiasm inspired those around him to follow his lead. They were all-in because he was.

He did not micromanage—he did not deal with assistant coaches on a daily basis and he certainly didn't call plays—but he worked side by side with his top executives to make sure their efforts were aligned with the vision and design he had set. With some, there was plenty of intellectual jousting about ideas, which forced every party to raise his game. He was available and accessible, but he also wanted people to feel comfortable to do their jobs without fear that he was looking over their shoulders.

My father's approach created a feeling of trust throughout the building. His employees felt they could create new approaches to their work and even engage and challenge the boss—and he would often challenge them back—with innovative thinking. He sought employees out to collaborate, too, and if someone needed him to make a call or intervene at a high level, he was well-known for getting it done quickly.

Finally, the people he hired to execute his plans were stellar. Chuck Noll, Bill Nunn and Joe Gordon—a coach, a scout, a public relations man—are still regarded as among the very best at what they did in the history of the NFL. My father and his brother Art clashed later, but in the 1960s, they together studied how the Packers, Giants and Bears scouted college football players and that became the foundation of the Steelers' scouting process in the 1970s. He made his sister-in-law, Geraldine Glenn, one of the first female executives in NFL history by putting her in charge of the ticket operation. Together, this management team was so in tune and operating at such a high level that, I believe, it likely could have successfully run any type of business.

From his initial vision and design for success to the people he hired to help him implement them, the Steelers of the 1970s were the proving ground for my father's core business practices and principles.

FIVE

DYNASTY

THE PITTSBURGH STEELERS OF THE 1970S became, and remain, one of the great dynasties in American sports history. All these years later, the team's success almost seems taken for granted, as if those four Super Bowl titles in six seasons were inevitable, given the extraordinary talent the Steelers had on and off the field.

The truth is, nobody really saw that success coming. Certainly not in 1968, when the Steelers stumbled through a dismal 2-11-1 season led by Bill Austin, a coach who had been hired primarily because he was Vince Lombardi's buddy. Austin's record in three seasons was 11-28-3 and it was obvious that another coaching change was necessary. And it had to be done right.

Strong, successful organizations generally have stability at the top. The Steelers had just one owner but went through 16 head coaches from the first season in 1933 through 1968, which meant they were changing coaches almost every other year. Only two—Jock Sutherland and Buddy Parker—compiled winning records.

That instability simply couldn't be sustained, not in the new NFL that was emerging as a result of the NFL-AFL consolidation that began in the late 1960s. The league was on the verge of becoming a global business and a cultural phenomenon. If the Steelers wanted to be something more than an afterthought, they needed the kind of success that can flow from consistent leadership.

So the search for yet another new head coach began. This time, though, Dan took over the search and he was determined to give the job to the best candidate, not someone who was a friend of a friend. Leading a coaching search was something my father had never done before and he would never have to do much more afterward. In the next four-plus decades, he'd hire just three coaches. None was fired, and each won at least one Super Bowl.

Dan Rooney knew exactly what he was looking for in a head coach. He wanted someone who shared his philosophy of team building but who would not be a yes-man. He wanted someone who would bring order and a systematic approach to putting together the roster and managing the team, acting not only as the head coach but also as the de facto general manager, with responsibility for the draft and the roster. Every part of the operation would be a meritocracy, with jobs going to those who showed ability, without relying on connections, reputation or race.

On the day after Super Bowl III—the momentous Joe Namath guarantee game—Dan met with one of the losing coaches. Chuck Noll was listed as the defensive backfield coach for Don Shula's Baltimore Colts, but he was running the entire defense. My mother remembers my father's reaction to him after their initial two-hour meeting.

"He loved him from the minute he met him," she said. "He came home and said, 'I think we got our guy.' That was the first meeting."

Noll and Dan were kindred spirits. They were both 35 and had somewhat similar personal histories. My mother describes them as having "gentle" backgrounds, with good parents, good families, good education and their faith. Noll grew up in poverty, in an area of Cleveland that was racially mixed and, like my father, he had always been comfortable working and living with people of different backgrounds.

"Chuck absolutely did not see color," said Noll's widow, Marianne. She remembers Noll telling her of a time when he was reading aloud a pre-draft scouting report with his assistant coaches, reviewing what a player could or could not do. One of the assistants asked what color the player was and Noll had no idea.

Noll had played messenger guard for Paul Brown in Cleveland. While there, he went to law school. And after his playing days ended, Noll worked for Sid Gillman at the AFL's Los Angeles Chargers. Finally, in the mid-1960s, he joined the Baltimore Colts' staff and quickly became Shula's protégé.

Noll and Rooney saw running a football team through the same lens. They shared a vision of how a successful organization should look and behave. At that first meeting, Noll surprised Rooney with insight into the Steelers that Dan had assumed only insiders would know. And Noll's design for how he would shape the Steelers aligned perfectly with Dan Rooney's ideas. They both wanted to bring structure to the team. They both believed in doing what was right, but also in setting high standards—and then getting others to follow them to reach those goals.

Noll believed in stocking the roster through the draft, getting young, self-motivated players and then teaching them how to play. He noted that the Steelers had made a habit of trading away their draft picks. And he was candid. He told my father the Steelers would have to be patient, that there was no quick fix. The vision shared by Noll and Rooney was clear: The team had to be rebuilt and a winning culture had to be established. It was not an overnight job and simply being a good team would not be enough for Noll. Noll wanted to win championships.

It was everything Dan Rooney wanted to hear, in part because it was everything he had thought to be true, too. I don't think my father had as much professional and personal synergy with any other partner in his career as he had with Noll. They shared many fundamental philosophies. A voracious reader, Noll was enamored with learning. He loved to fly, and in fact encouraged Dan's passion for aviation. He believed that well-rounded men made better players because they were better equipped to face challenges, so he wanted his players to go home by 6 p.m.

Dan Rooney knew right away that Noll would make him better, and that feeling empowered him. They had a mutual sense of purpose. Noll, Rooney thought, would bring a sense of professionalism and excellence to the organization. They were, in short, very much alike.

"The way he did it was with dignity," Dan once said about Noll. "His players were always his concern, both in treating them well and giving them what they needed to succeed on the field. He set a new standard for the Steelers that still is the foundation of what we do and who we are. From the players to the coaches to the front office down to the ball boys, he taught us all what it took to be a winner."

Still, my father was adamant about conducting a systematic search, so he interviewed other candidates. But after a few more interviews with Noll—including one at my family's home when Noll's son played with my older brothers and sisters and my mom talked to Marianne about schools and housing—Charles Henry Noll was hired late in January 1969. At his first press conference, it was noted that he was the 14th head coach in the team's 36-year history. Dan Rooney particularly loved Noll's answer when he was asked why he thought he was the one who could end the years of losing in Pittsburgh.

"Losing has nothing to do with geography," Noll responded.

My mother says that when Noll showed up, he brought magic with him. He was the first member of Dan Rooney's management team, and that was fitting. Dan had already put the infrastructure of the franchise in place, but Noll was the perfect person to implement and complement Dan Rooney's plans.

Before the other people who would help Dan Rooney build the Steelers could be put in place—before Noll even had a chance to unpack in Pittsburgh— the college draft began, just a few days after Noll was hired. Noll was Dan Rooney's first building block. He and Noll would immediately have to decide on the second.

Noll, as Shula's assistant, had been scouting players in the 1969 college class, and a looming defensive tackle from North Texas State had caught his eye. Joe Greene was, at 6-foot-4 and 275 pounds, a natural athlete and a ferocious competitor. He had grown up without a father in the central Texas city of Temple, and his mother worked long hours as a housekeeper for white families. As a kid, Greene picked cotton and pecans, and when he grew bigger, he also worked construction jobs. His high school—Dunbar, the school for black children in his town—played their football games on Thursdays or Saturdays in Temple. Friday nights were reserved for the white high schools. Greene graduated high school in 1965. The widespread desegregation of Texas' public schools did not start until a few years later.

Greene was not heavily recruited as a high schooler. Dunbar had not been a good team despite his presence, and the Southwest Conference—dominated by the powerhouse Texas Longhorns and Arkansas Razorbacks and including many of the big schools in Texas—had not yet integrated. He landed at North Texas State. There, Greene picked up the nickname "Mean Joe"—Greene was sensitive and did not like the tag—because of his relentless play and because North Texas State's team was known as "The Mean Green." During the three seasons in which he played defensive tackle, the Mean Green were 23-15-1, and during those 39 games, their opponents were held to fewer than 2 yards per carry. In his senior year, Greene was a consensus All-American. Noll thought Greene would not just be a great player, but the leader his rebuilding team needed. Noll wanted Greene to be the Steelers' first-round pick.

At the same time, there was considerable public pressure and some internal support for the Steelers to draft a local boy, Terry Hanratty, a Notre Dame quarterback who had grown up in Butler, just an hour north of Pittsburgh. In a previous era, such a sentiment—based on emotions and connections and factors other than football—might have carried the day.

But Dan Rooney had made crystal clear his design. Every facet of the Steelers organization would be grounded in merit. It was how Noll became the first head coach he hired and it would be how draft decisions would be weighed.

Noll knew how he wanted his team to play. He would not be nudged off his plan by personal appeals. "In order to win a game, you have to first not lose it," he often said. In other words, Noll was determined to build the defense up first. The Steelers would have a Steel Curtain.

Noll also had an important backer. Dan believed strongly that the coach had to have the final say over the roster, so he supported Noll's plans for the draft.

Greene was Noll's first pick. Hanratty was still available in the second round and the Steelers took him, too. The NFL draft is a much bigger event now than it was then. But the reaction to Noll's first draft pick drew the ire of the local media. The next day's headline in The Pittsburgh Press was blunt: "Who's Joe Greene?"

It was, of course, a momentous pick, not just because of what Greene would become—nothing less than the cornerstone of a dynasty and a member of the Pro Football Hall of Fame—but because of what he symbolized in that moment about the Steelers' intentions.

"We are doing what we think is best and we are not worried about reputation, we are not worried about selling tickets, we are not worried about anything but what we think is best," Tony Dungy, who would become a Steeler several years later, said of the signal the pick sent about the Steelers' philosophy. "This small school, unknown, black defensive tackle, we are going to take ahead of the local, white quarterback from the biggest football powerhouse in the country. That to me is a defining moment."

Dan had a visceral connection to Greene. He simply hated to lose—Noll called it Greene's "singleness of purpose"—and it rubbed off on the other players, including future Hall of Famers the Steelers would add in ensuing years. Greene could be nasty when the team did lose. And he had a presence about him. My father had been around players since he was a small child, but there was never a player like Greene to him. He was the guy my dad always dreamed a quintessential Steeler would be like, and they built a close relationship. Greene was tough and smart and a remarkable leader. To Dan Rooney, Greene was the embodiment of what he and Noll had set out to build. Greene was a Steeler and, within a few years, the Steelers would be Super Bowl champions. Greene was the living confirmation that their approach worked.

Greene's presence also indicated a sea change in the mindset of the Steelers. For years, NFL teams put colored dots next to player names on their internal draft boards. Some dots indicated players who had injuries. Other dots indicated the race of the player. The race-related dots had been on the Steelers' draft board before Noll arrived. With Rooney now fully in charge of the football team, and with Noll sharing his views, those dots were removed, signaling to everybody working for the Steelers that the men at the top were serious about establishing a meritocracy.

Just as telling was who was collaborating behind the scenes with Noll and Rooney as they prepared for the draft. Among those who advised Noll to ignore the demands for Hanratty and select Greene was a part-time scout named Bill Nunn Jr.

Nunn was a Pittsburgh native who had played college basketball at West Virginia State. As a side job, he wrote press releases about the school's football team.

Journalism was Nunn's family business. His father was William Nunn Sr., managing editor of the Pittsburgh Courier, one of the leading African-American newspapers in the country. That job gave Nunn Sr. a huge platform, and he used it to push for integration of blacks into the military, to advocate for the integration of Major League Baseball and to raise funds to help an attorney for the National Association for the Advancement of Colored People argue a case before the United States Supreme Court in 1954. That attorney, Thurgood Marshall, won the case—Brown v. Board of Education, which ruled that "separate but equal" education in public schools was unconstitutional.

Nunn Jr. began his journalism career as an intern, working with Wendell Smith, the famed Courier writer who traced Jackie Robinson's entrance into Major League Baseball. After Nunn graduated in 1948, he turned down a spot on the Harlem Globetrotters and went to work as a sports reporter at the Courier.

Nunn worked his way up to sports editor and eventually, after his father's retirement in the mid-1960s, to managing editor. He was best known, though, for his coverage of college football, particularly in the South, where teams—reflecting the Jim Crow laws of the era—were segregated. Most of the big state schools and private colleges south of the Mason-Dixon Line had all-white football teams, and the region's media coverage mostly ignored teams and players from the schools that did have black players.

Nunn carved out that beat for himself.

He wrote about HBCUs like Southern, Arkansas A&M, Grambling, Alcorn State and Alabama A&M. He chose a black All-Star team, and at the end of each season, he selected what came to be regarded as the definitive All-America team for black colleges and celebrated those players at a banquet in Pittsburgh.

He was so close to and so respected by the HBCUs that their coaches, like Grambling's legendary Eddie Robinson, stayed at Nunn's home when they came north for recruiting. As a result, Nunn knew more about who the best black players were than practically anyone else. Even white scouts for opposing teams acknowledged that coaches like Robinson told Nunn things about players that he did not tell them. Nunn, almost single-handedly, put black players on the radars of NFL and AFL scouts and coaches as teams were beginning to reintegrate their rosters in the 1950s and 1960s.

An example of Nunn's influence: In 1953, Wellington Mara, the owner of the New York Giants, instructed his team to use its 27th-round pick on a tackle from Morgan State College named Roosevelt Brown. In his hand, legend has it, Mara held a copy of the Courier's All-America team, compiled by Nunn. Mara pointed to Brown's name in the paper and told his staff, "Take this guy." Brown was the Giants' starting left tackle for 13 seasons, an All-Pro for six of them.

The Steelers, though, rarely drafted the players Nunn wrote about and Nunn noticed. Like most NFL teams at that time, the Steelers had no mechanism in place for scouting the HBCUs. They focused on the big universities, and because those teams were overwhelmingly white, the Steelers didn't see many black players at all.

In the 1960s, the Steelers' offices were at the Roosevelt Hotel in a section of the city now called the Cultural District. Long before media access to football teams was restricted by rules and layers of gatekeepers, it was routine for local reporters and editors to stop by to chat. (Until the very end of his life, my father would stroll into the media workroom at the Steelers' training facility to chat with the beat reporters.) In 1967, Dan had been reading Nunn's column and was curious about his All-America team. One day, Dan asked Rick Roberts, a Courier writer who covered the Steelers, why his editor—Bill Nunn Jr.—rarely came around.

The Nunn and Rooney families were not strangers. My grandfather had played baseball on the sandlots with Nunn Sr., who had played for the Homestead Grays. And when the Steelers traveled to the South for games during the 1950s, Nunn Sr. helped my grandfather find housing for black Steelers players.

When Dan's question was relayed to him, Nunn Jr. did not hold back. He told Roberts to be sure to tell Dan Rooney that he didn't have to worry about him coming down to the Steelers office, because he did not like the way the Steelers or the NFL did business. My father didn't get mad. He got interested. The Steelers were struggling badly then and my father, already thinking of what he could change to improve the team, wanted to hear what had turned Nunn off about how the Steelers worked.

My father called Nunn and asked if they could meet, along with my grandfather. Nunn gave them a lot to think about during that conversation. Nunn told Dan that while an earlier Steelers coach, Buddy Parker, had attended the banquet for the black college football All-Americans and stayed for hours talking football, the coach at the time, Bill Austin, skipped the event entirely and so did the rest of the organization. Nunn would hear from other NFL teams about the players on his All-America team, but never the Steelers. Nunn said he even felt personally unwelcome when he went to the press box at games because he represented a black paper.

"I don't think you'll ever be a winner," he told Dan Rooney.

Dan offered Nunn a job on the spot, asking him to come help make the Steelers winners. When Nunn replied that he already had a job, Dan asked him to work part-time for the Steelers. Nunn was covering a game every week at the time, and my father asked him if he would start writing up reports on the players he saw.

That is how Nunn came to work for the Steelers in 1967, and how he was in a position to advise Noll to take Greene with his first draft pick. Soon after Noll was hired in 1969, Nunn went to work for the Steelers full time, working with my uncle, Art Rooney Jr., who ran the personnel department

Noll, Nunn and Rooney were philosophically aligned and they understood immediately the advantage Nunn was delivering. My father was an idealist. He wanted badly to have a successful team that was also a model of integration, and he had made that clear to his top football people. Nunn was helping to deliver that. If Nunn were working today, he would not just be considered a top scout. His role today would also be called the team's chief of diversity and inclusion. In addition, he and my father became good friends and shared interests beyond football, from local politics to the history of the Pittsburgh region.

Nunn worked for the Steelers for 46 years in all. He suffered the stroke that took his life while analyzing college players at the Steelers' offices just weeks before the 2014 draft. The room at the Steelers' headquarters where they conduct the draft each year is named for him. And there is a bench honoring Nunn high on a hill overlooking the practice fields at Saint Vincent College, in the spot where Nunn used to hold court during training camp.

The real monument to Nunn, though, was his impact on the Steelers and the entire NFL. Of all the people Dan Rooney hired in his life—including three Super Bowl-winning coaches—none may have been as transformational as Nunn. His presence gave the Steelers tremendous credibility among black players and college coaches as a premier, forward-thinking organization. And it was another signal to players and coaches of all ethnicities that, philosophically, Dan Rooney believed diversity—of background and thought—would improve the team.

And Nunn gave the Steelers access to the gold mine of talent at HBCUs.

Before Nunn joined the Steelers full time in 1969, the team had not drafted any players from the HBCUs in the previous two seasons. Within three years of the start of Nunn's tenure, the Steelers had drafted a total of 14 players from those schools. From 1969 to 1975, the Steelers drafted 25 players from the schools—more than any other team in the NFL and twice the league average.

That did not even include undrafted free agents or players acquired by trade.

The Steelers had their greatest draft—the greatest in NFL history—in 1974. Picking 21st in the draft order, the Steelers selected four future Hall of Famers: Lynn Swann, Jack Lambert, John Stallworth and Mike Webster. Stallworth had played for Alabama A&M. Undrafted that year and signed as a free agent was a 5-foot-11 defensive back from South Carolina State, Donnie Shell.

"So many of the black players got there because of Bill," said Tony Dungy, who came to the Steelers as a defensive back in 1977. "Not getting drafted, Donnie didn't know what to do, so he talked to his coach and when he asked his coach what he should do, his coach had a relationship with Bill. He said, go to the Steelers. You're going to be treated fairly. You'll get an opportunity."

Shell played 14 seasons for the Steelers, was an All-Pro three times and won four Super Bowls.

Like any business in the throes of an organizational overhaul, it took several years for the team to hit its stride. My father hated to lose at anything, but he was able to balance his own frustration with the team's struggles against the view of the big picture. He also knew he couldn't get that upset over one loss, or even one bad season. His vision for the franchise stretched far beyond the record in one or two seasons. Later in life, when he sat in a box at Heinz Field with members of the Steelers' brain trust during games, he was not prone to big outbursts. He was a fan like the rest of us, capable of banging the table and questioning a play call. But most often, he would stand in the back of the box, with little expression, his hands in his pockets—in full view of reporters, who were sitting in the press box separated only by a pane of glass.

Eventually the results of that infusion from the new pipeline of talent became clear, and the belief in patiently building through the draft paid off.

The Steelers' winning percentage jumped dramatically, from 7.1 percent in 1969—Noll had been right that there was no quick fix—to 78.6 in 1972, the Steelers' first winning season under Noll. From 1972 to 1979, the Steelers led the league in victories, averaging 11 wins each regular season, with a winning record of 76.1 percent.

From 1972 to 1979, the Steelers led the league in the number of postseason games with 18, and also had the most postseason wins during that span—14 total—including six division wins, four conference championships and, of course, four Super Bowls within six seasons, a record that still stands. A straight line can be drawn between Dan Rooney's push for a more diverse roster and the Steelers' winning percentage.

Of the 29 players drafted between 1969 and 1976 who were voted into the Pro Football Hall of Fame, nine played for the Steelers. No other team had more than two players drafted in that span go into the Hall of Fame. Of the 29, six came from HBCUs and two of those six were Steelers—Mel Blount (Southern) and John Stallworth (Alabama A&M). Just as Greene had come to embody what Rooney envisioned a Steelers player to be, Blount and Stallworth represented his vision for how diversity in every part of the franchise—from the scout hired from an African-American newspaper because of his expertise in HBCUs to the players he helped discover—would vault the Steelers ahead of their competition.

The success of players from those schools was not limited to Pittsburgh. Draft picks for all teams selected between 1969 and 1976 from the HBCUs started more games on average than players from other schools (45.32 games to 37.68), had more time as a primary starter for their team (3.31 years to 2.8), created more sacks (an average of 15.86 sacks per player from an HBCU in his career to 8.99 for a player from a non-HBCU) and scored more touchdowns (an average of 9.23 per player from an HBCU to 6.13 from a non-HBCU).

As the bigger schools, particularly in the South, integrated in the late 1960s and 1970s, the doors were opened for the top black high school football players to head there. Because most teams still put most of their efforts into scouting those schools, those players were more firmly on NFL radars than they would have been before integration. The University of Texas had its first African-American player in 1970. A year later, the University of Alabama followed suit. (John Mitchell, who would go on to be a longtime Steelers assistant, was the first African-American player to play for Bear Bryant.)

Integration of the South's most successful college football programs may have cut into the initial edge the Steelers had in the first half of the 1970s from their efforts to get players from the HBCUs. But Nunn was also crucial in establishing a culture at the Steelers that helped them navigate the turbulent times. He was trusted by the team's black players and became a sounding board for them. And, because he became such a trusted confidant and advisor to Dan, he could offer players insight about what the organization was doing while also giving the top management a heads-up if a player might create a challenge. Nunn set up training camp at Saint Vincent College every summer and he started a program to encourage team bonding. Nunn would pair a veteran player with a younger player in the dorm rooms for camp. The veterans were not always thrilled with the matching program. Shell remembers complaining to Nunn about always getting rookies as roommates. Then, in 1977, a young defensive back from the University of Minnesota arrived. Nunn told Shell, "You can help Tony Dungy."

Shell credits Nunn's program with building a family atmosphere at the Steelers, and that was a critical piece of Rooney's vision for how the Steelers would do business and treat people. He wanted people at the Steelers to take pride in working there so that they would want to do their best for the team—whether they were selling tickets or sacking a quarterback. Stallworth, one of the gems Nunn discovered, remembers a picture taken at a dinner after the Steelers won Super Bowl XIV, the fourth Super Bowl won in six seasons.

Noll had been walking around with Nunn to different tables, stopping to talk to the players at each table. He got to the table where Stallworth was sitting with his wife. In the photo, Noll was standing while talking to Stallworth and Nunn is standing a little bit back from Noll.

"The look on Bill's face was that he looked like a proud papa," Stallworth said. "He looked about as proud as he could be about his role in my coming, but maybe in a greater way, his role in a lot of us coming from HBCUs.

Along with Noll, Nunn had helped Rooney accomplish one of his top professional priorities, constructing a team that embraced players of all races, with every emphasis on ability, and proving that it was the best formula for success.

For that, Nunn, who never played or coached football, was made an inaugural member of the Black College Football Hall of Fame in 2010. And he was nominated for the Pro Football Hall of Fame in 2007.

Blount believes the success of the Steelers in the 1970s can be traced to the relationship among my father, Noll and Nunn. Blount knew of black players on other NFL teams who had come from HBCUs who never felt comfortable in their own locker rooms among their teammates and coaches.

Noll was the first white coach Blount had ever had and, with the Steelers, Blount had the first white teammates of his life. But he doesn't remember ever feeling out of place with the Steelers. Greene says racial discrimination was simply not an issue with the Steelers. In his own book, Dan Rooney wrote that Nunn paid him one of the greatest compliments of his life when he told another team executive that "I don't think Dan sees color. And I don't say that about a lot of people."

Dan Rooney and Noll had made it clear—they would do what was best for the team, no matter who it involved. Noll, himself, had not been a star player. He was undersized as an offensive lineman, and he rejected the idea that players should play because they fit a type or because of how high they were drafted. They would play based only on how they performed.

SIX

CREATING THE STEELERS BRAND

THE MERIT-BASED APPROACH DAN ROONEY HAD HOPED FOR when he hired Chuck Noll was never on fuller display than at the start of the 1974 season. The Steelers had finally turned the corner. They had been to the playoffs the previous two seasons; Terry Bradshaw had been the starting quarterback for the last four.

But Bradshaw did not have a stranglehold on the job any more than anyone else did. Joe Gilliam was an All-American at Tennessee State, an HBCU that was named the black college national champion in Gilliam's junior and senior seasons of 1970 and 1971. The Steelers drafted Gilliam in the 11th round in 1972. He performed well in the 1974 preseason, well enough for Noll to name him the starter. Even Bradshaw would later say Gilliam had been better.

Gilliam's ascension reverberated far beyond Pittsburgh and even the NFL. Gilliam was the first black quarterback in the history of the league to be named the starter prior to the season—and he had done it by supplanting the first overall draft pick who had helped engineer the franchise's turnaround. Before Gilliam, only two African-American quarterbacks—Marlin Briscoe and James Harris—had gotten significant playing time for any NFL team.

The Gilliam decision was a groundbreaker and the Steelers became national news. Gilliam's photo was on the cover of Sports Illustrated with the headline "Pittsburgh's Black Quarterback."

Gilliam received hate mail and death threats. Mike Wagner had the locker next to Gilliam's and he would read some of the mail.

"It was all hate," Wagner said. "I didn't know how to react to it. I would sit next to him, and I would just go, 'Oh, geez, Joe. This is terrible.' "

The temptation was to think that Noll and the Steelers were trying to make a social statement with the choice of Gilliam. They were not. But the decision to start Gilliam meant a great deal to the black players on the team. It spoke powerfully to them, Shell said, about opportunity and what the Steelers stood for. The players felt that their dignity was being respected because the team was willing to choose a black quarterback after a fair competition. It enhanced the level of trust between the black players and management and, perhaps most important, it convinced people that Rooney, Noll and Nunn were not just paying lip service to equal opportunity and merit.

The trust that had been built eased the disappointment when, after the sixth game of the season, with the Steelers' record at 4-1-1 but with Gilliam struggling off the field and not following the game plan on it, Noll put Bradshaw back in. Dan agreed with the decision. He thought Noll had given Gilliam every chance and he appreciated Gilliam's strong arm and hard work. Pulling him was difficult, and there were players in the locker room who thought Noll was making a mistake. But Joe Greene thought Bradshaw was the best leader for the team. And Noll's decisions on Gilliam changed some players' perspectives on the white coaches—Noll would not deviate from the meritocracy, and he would play whoever he thought could win.

"I believe that Chuck gave Joe Gilliam every opportunity to be successful," Joe Greene said. "He tried to help Joe as best he could because when he made a decision to put Joe in, he made a decision to put Joe in because he felt Joe was the best guy for us at the time to win. It had nothing to do with race. Same way, when he took Joe out. It was because Joe didn't live up to his expectations at that time, and he was having a hard time. He put Bradshaw back in, and he stayed in. I never saw it as a race issue."

The Steelers went on to win their first Super Bowl, Super Bowl IX, that year, manhandling the Minnesota Vikings, 16-6. Franco Harris rushed for 158 yards and a touchdown. Terry Bradshaw threw a touchdown pass on a play that, legend has it, was suggested on the sideline by Gilliam. Noll's defense forced five turnovers and held the Vikings to just 119 yards of offense. It was the first of four championships the Steelers won in a six-year span.

My grandfather wanted my father to accept that first Lombardi Trophy from Pete Rozelle, but my father resisted. He wanted my grandfather to be rewarded for founding the team, for staying in Pittsburgh, for getting through difficult financial times. But my father, who lived to celebrate all six Super Bowl championships, always said that the first one was still the sweetest.

Dan Rooney had hoped to build a stable, successful business when he began to run the Steelers. He and his team wound up creating the new NFL's first dynasty.

At the heart of it stood Greene, the emotional counterweight to Noll's straightforward, more analytical approach. Rooney, Nunn and Noll worked hard at building a winning culture at the Steelers, but it was Greene who brought all of their best intentions to life. He was a natural leader—and eventually the team captain—and he was the greatest player in Steelers history. He played 91 straight games and he missed just nine games in his 13-year career. He was the Defensive Player of the Year twice, was voted first-team All-Pro five times and was a first-ballot Hall of Famer in 1987. My father held him in such high regard that when he was elected to the Pro Football Hall of Fame in 2000, he chose Greene to present him at the enshrinement ceremony.

There was one moment from the 1970 season—Greene's second—that Dan particularly cherished. By his own admission, Greene was volatile when he was a young player. It was the final game of the regular season, and the Steelers were about to lose in Philadelphia to finish the season 5-9. It was a four-game improvement from the previous season, but the Steelers still had a long way to go. In frustration, Greene hurled the football into the stands.

Dan Rooney was no fan of drama or bad behavior, but Greene once overheard my father tell my grandfather, "If someone could do that, and winning means that much to him, we need that kind of attitude on this team." As Greene said 11 years later when he was in Rooney's office telling him that he was going to retire at the end of the 1981 season, my father brought that moment up. Greene couldn't believe it. He thought that after all those years, Dan was unhappy he had thrown the football. Instead, my father said, "When you did that, I felt the same way."

Greene became the locker room disciplinarian, setting a standard with his own expectations for himself and others. He would often spend his time in interviews praising lesser-known players as a way to encourage and support them. He befriended Terry Bradshaw, who—as a child of the segregated South— had never before been in a workplace where blacks and whites toiled together. Bradshaw has talked openly about being anxious and overwhelmed when he was a young player, the first overall pick of the 1970 draft. It was Greene who recognized that the Steelers would win with Bradshaw and who reassured him that he would be critical to the Steelers winning.

But Greene would also lead by intimidation when he had to. He would silence complainers with just a glare. On the Monday before the 1974 AFC Championship game in Oakland, several rookies on the team, including Stallworth, asked the team's equipment manager for some spare boxes. They were already planning for when the season would end and they would have to pack up their lockers.

The implication was clear—the players weren't sure the Steelers were going to win in Oakland. Greene would not have that.

Greene asked the rookies why they wanted the boxes. Wisely, nobody answered. He asked them a second time. Again, silence. The message had been delivered.

Dan Rooney understood that everybody in any line of work watches the top boss, and in this case that was him. So he was careful to behave in a way that signaled what he wanted his business to represent. He stood in the same cafeteria line with the players and secretaries and media members. He was in the locker room after every game—win or lose—to shake players' hands. He went to the opponents' locker rooms, too, to greet their owners. After particularly bad losses, Dan would walk the aisle of the team plane saying nothing, merely to show players and coaches that he was not raving mad. Dan Rooney didn't brag, but he had tremendous confidence in himself. He believed he knew how to build a successful program, and he felt even more sure that the Steelers were on the right path when Noll arrived.

Rooney was proud of how he was running the team and I was particularly proud of him. When the Steelers beat the Cowboys to win Super Bowl XIII, my grandfather did not go to the podium to receive the Lombardi Trophy from Rozelle. Dan Rooney went alone. My grandfather deserves credit for the Steelers' esprit de corps and the organization's commitment toward treating people with respect. But he was not a great manager and he knew it. My father was, and I knew how hard he worked at it, how on Christmas morning we would open our presents at 7 a.m. so he could be in his office by 9—even though, of course, the owner had the prerogative to stay home on Christmas. But he put everything he had into the Steelers, and it was why all the skilled, smart people around him followed his lead. So even though I was still a young boy that day in Miami's old Orange Bowl, watching my father receive the trophy meant a lot to me.

Dan Rooney was elected to the Pro Football Hall of Fame primarily because of his acumen with the league's affairs and with the football operations of the team. His day job, though, was running the business of the Pittsburgh Steelers.

From cost management to marketing to negotiating player contracts, Dan Rooney didn't just turn around the team's fortunes on the field—he elevated the Steelers into one of the most popular and respected brands in the NFL. And he sustained it for nearly 50 years.

The Steelers play in one of the smallest markets in American professional sports. But the Steelers are recognized worldwide, just like the Yankees and Dodgers are. That was not always the case. It took years of winning football and strategic planning to elevate the Steelers' recognizability well beyond their small geographic area.

Among the first things travelers see after landing at Pittsburgh International Airport are side-by-side life-size statues. One is of George Washington in full military uniform. It commemorates the occasion in 1754 when, in western Pennsylvania, a young Washington fired the first shots of the French and Indian War.

Next to him is a rendering of no less an iconic figure. Crouched over, his hands nearly grazing the floor, is Franco Harris, the Steelers' Hall of Fame running back. Harris was at the center of what might have been the single most important play in Steelers history and one of the most famous plays in all of the NFL.

In 1972, after nearly 40 years of failure, the Steelers were in the postseason as the champions of the AFC's Central Division. Two days before Christmas, the Steelers hosted the Raiders at Three Rivers Stadium. And the Steelers were about to lose. They were trailing 7-5 with 22 seconds and no timeouts left and facing fourth-and-10 from their own 40-yard line. Bradshaw had been forced out of the pocket by the Raiders' pass rush, forcing him to improvise and abandon the play called in the huddle, a pass for wide receiver Barry Pearson. Instead, he threw a pass intended for running back Frenchy Fuqua down the middle of the field. There was a collision between Fuqua and the Raiders' famously fierce safety Jack Tatum. The ball ricocheted backward toward the line of scrimmage, and somehow Harris, who had started downfield in case Bradshaw needed another pass option, scooped up the carom off his shoe tops and rumbled for the winning touchdown.

The Steelers lost the conference championship game the following week to the Miami Dolphins, whose coach, Don Shula, was Noll's mentor. But the Immaculate Reception, as Harris' amazing play was christened, represents the turning point in Steelers lore, exorcising a history of losing that stretched back to the founding of the team. Like that football flying end over end toward Harris, the Steelers were hurtling toward greatness.

At the same time, what we now call Steelers Nation was being constructed with the help of my father's most important business partner, longtime public relations executive Joe Gordon. Rooney and Gordon, who was hired shortly after Noll, would shape the image of the Steelers and broaden their fan base far beyond their relatively small hometown. At the beginning, Gordon and Rooney wanted to make sure that the community and the way the Steelers did business got the same kind of recognition as teams from bigger cities did. As the NFL's popularity exploded, they did not want the Steelers to become an afterthought, but always to be viewed as leaders.

Gordon was as important to building the business of the Steelers as Noll was to building the football team. He became Rooney's closest collaborator in what we would now call marketing and branding.

In the 1970s, though, NFL teams did not have sprawling departments with sophisticated plans devoted to spreading the word about the teams. Gordon was a one-man band, arranging interviews and sponsorship deals, booking player appearances and always keeping an eye on what was being written and said about the team, all while pecking away with one finger on his typewriter to produce notes about the team while he talked to reporters in his office at the same time.

Rooney and Gordon were a perfect match because while they would argue, they did not compete with each other. My father did not seek to constrain Gordon or to see only his own ideas go forward. He created an environment where, as with his other executives, he and Gordon could freely share their ideas and hash them out, trusting that the best ones would rise to the top. It was an environment in which someone as talented and with as much vision as Gordon—just like Noll or Nunn—would flourish.

More than once, Rooney and Gordon would loudly challenge each other behind closed doors, debating what was best for the team. Minutes later, they would emerge, laughing, and go to lunch.

Most of Gordon's ideas and innovations were designed to broaden the Steelers' fan base beyond Pittsburgh. Among the first things he did was invite the beat writers from the small suburban papers surrounding Pittsburgh—outlets as far east as Altoona, down into West Virginia, from Beaver Falls to McKeesport to Uniontown—to travel on the team charter to away games. Gordon knew that many people in the surrounding towns did not read the big newspapers from Pittsburgh—the Post-Gazette and the Press—but instead got their news from their local paper. Those papers all had people who covered the team during the week and at home games, but they could not afford to send writers on the road. So the Steelers took them with the team, including to Super Bowls.

Gordon and my father spoke every night about everything that was written and said about the Steelers in the media. They discussed which reporters they could trust, which ones understood Noll best, which ones had no idea how the business worked. They talked about themes for stories they wanted to pitch to media members.

Gordon, who shared my dad's vision of a franchise that would represent its hometown and stand for something more than just a diversion, worked hard to shape the way the team was portrayed. He developed personal relationships with media members and let them know if he thought they were going astray. He even once told a longtime Pittsburgh television and radio personality, Stan Savran—who, like Gordon, is Jewish—that he should not work on the High Holy Days.

Each week of the football season, Gordon sat at his typewriter and wrote thumbnail biographies—just a few sentences—on each player to give to the network television announcer crews. That kind of preparation is standard now but was revolutionary then. And it helped those broadcasting Steelers games inject statistics and personal notes during games, which not only made the broadcasters look plugged in, but also cast the team's personnel in a positive light.

Gordon had already impressed upon the players—including the stars—the role the media played in the business of the Steelers and the NFL. He had the ear of players in part because he was also responsible for setting up endorsement deals and speaking engagements. So when he told a player to meet a reporter in the hotel lobby, the player made sure he was in the lobby on time.

Dan Rooney was closely involved with most of Gordon's efforts. For instance, Dan cared a lot about the game day program—selling ads for it was one of his early jobs with the team. When he and Gordon sat down at one of their first meetings, Dan went over every detail—what stories and photos he liked to see in it, what size the ads should be, what font should be used. Gordon was shocked not only by how much my father knew about publishing, but also by how engaged he was on a project that most owners never think about. Dan brought that level of enthusiasm and immersive interest to everything to do with the Steelers. Gordon said it inspired him and others who worked for Dan Rooney to raise their games to match him.

Perhaps because Gordon was a Pittsburgh native and my family was so closely entwined with the community—my grandfather and later my father both walked to work and to home games among throngs of fans—the Steelers were proactive about having players appear at community events. Dan Rooney was intent on having the team represent something special. He wanted to provide fans a good community experience. It was, as Gordon describes it, by design, but it also came naturally to treat fans and media in a respectful, friendly way.

The Steelers' style of play fit neatly with the blue-collar image of the city. The team was not glamorous like Joe Namath's Jets. It was tough, built on defense, intent on burying opponents and winning the war of attrition. As a result, the Steelers resonated with people who identified as the hardworking little guys trying to do the right thing.

Gordon's eye for what would create and maintain a bond with fans was never greater than when a local radio promotion during the 1975 playoffs took off. Management at the radio station that had the Steelers' rights told Myron Cope, the color commentator on game broadcasts and host of the city's most popular sports talk show, that it wanted to create a gimmick to attract sponsors. Rooney didn't like the idea. He hated all gimmicks—many years later, he rolled his eyes at the advent of the team mascot, Steely McBeam. However, during a brain-storming session at the radio station, someone mentioned that the Miami Dolphins had a "Horrible Hankie," a white piece of fabric that fans waved at games. Cope liked the idea. He implored fans to bring any yellow or black towels to the game and wave them at critical moments in the action. The Terrible Towel—yellow, with black lettering—was eventually born, ready for its debut in the playoffs that December.

"The timing was like catching lightning in a bottle," Gordon said.

With a big push from Gordon, who quickly recognized the towel was something unique that Steelers fans could latch onto, the Terrible Towel was about to become the battle flag of Pittsburgh. What Cope initially thought would be a one-game promotion had to be used for every playoff game, Gordon thought. The Steelers won their second Super Bowl that season, and the Terrible Towel was attached to it. The following year, the first official Terrible Towel went on the market and it has become an iconic piece of Pittsburgh's history, traveling with fans into fighter jets and the International Space Station and to the summit of Mount Everest. Proceeds from sales of the Terrible Towel have raised millions of dollars for the Allegheny Valley School, which provides care for people with physical and mental disabilities and where Cope's son Danny lived.

Today, at almost any Steelers game you can see thousands of yellow Terrible Towels being waved. Gordon had understood the value of the Terrible Towel as a symbol of passion for the Steelers and what they represented, and he boosted Cope and the towel as important figures for the Steelers.

The making of the Steelers as a national team was certainly by the design of Dan Rooney and Joe Gordon, but an unfortunate element of happenstance played a part in spreading the reach of passion for the Steelers, too. The Steelers were reaching their peak success on the field just as the steel industry collapsed in the 1970s and early 1980s. As mills closed, more than 150,000 people lost their jobs and the local economy cratered. Pittsburgh suffered a startling population drain as people—particularly young people—had to move to find work, the population of Pittsburgh alone dropping by nearly 20 percent between the censuses of 1970 and 1980. As a result, Steelers fans were dispersed throughout the country, especially to the booming Sun Belt areas of Florida, Arizona and California.

Those fans remained loyal to the team, because the Steelers were the readily accessible connection to their hometown and to the lives they left behind. And the team had come to embody the image of western Pennsylvania. Steelers road games in some parts of the country often look more as if the game is being played at the confluence of the Allegheny and Monongahela rivers, with thousands of fans dressed in Steelers jerseys (Greene and Lambert are still wildly popular) and twirling Terrible Towels. That scene has, in turn, boosted even more the Steelers' popularity on the road and their draw for television ratings that far exceed Pittsburgh's market size.

Dan Rooney's goal was for the Steelers to be an intrinsic part of and a reflection of their region while also being relevant far beyond it. The plans he and Gordon conjured and implemented—and hashed over in those daily, sometimes loud phone calls and meetings—made the Steelers a local obsession and an outsized presence on the NFL landscape, a small-market team with the same high profile as franchises in New York and Chicago. And the Steelers have stayed there, a stalwart presence on everything from the NFL's prime-time television schedule to its annual list of jersey sales.

With all of this success, the internal conflict about money and its impact was even more resonant with my father's work at the Steelers. He knew the prices of everything—the jersey, the hat, the winter coat—and when he saw thousands of dollars worth of team-branded gear on someone whose home might be worth less than $35,000, it upset him. He thought things should work, and if things were incongruent, if he felt there was exploitation from the team or the league, I think it sickened him. He wanted fans to root for the Steelers more than anything in the world, but when they were going above their budget to buy the newest style of Steelers hat, he felt we had crossed a line.

The incongruity my father sensed never completely faded.

My oldest brother, Art, who is now the Steelers' president, was our father's right-hand man in his later years and he eventually replaced our father in running the team. My father understood that my brother Art had to take the business in a direction far beyond what he had, just as he had to go well beyond what the Chief ever envisioned.

However, the foundation my father created has sustained extraordinarily well. Even 50 years after that transformation began, the Pittsburgh market is usually in the bottom of all 32 NFL franchises for population, but the Steelers regularly appear in top-rated regular season games. In 2018, four Steelers games were within the top 10 rated regular season games. In 2017, the Steelers appeared in the top-ranked regular season game of the season. In 2016, they were in the second-ranked game.

When Forbes Magazine did its annual ranking of each team's value in 2018, it listed the Steelers as worth $2.45 billion. That put the team 31st out of the world's top 50 football, baseball, basketball and soccer teams, far outpacing the size of the market it represents. A local market report released in 2017 gave context to the Steelers' reach. It indicated that while the Steelers play in the 22nd largest metropolitan statistical area in the United States, they ranked fourth among NFL teams in popularity with 11.3 million fans nationally. Incredibly, only about a third of Steelers fans reside in Pennsylvania.

There is little doubt that the turnaround on the field that began in the 1970s drove the team's popularity just as the NFL was ascending to the top of professional sports on television.

There are few metrics that are easier to understand or more telling than a win-loss column. For more than three decades, the Steelers' results were unsightly. But the overhaul that Dan Rooney engineered in the 1970s with the hiring of Chuck Noll and his pursuit of a more diverse team resulted in success that was both dramatic and enduring.

As noted, through the contribution of Bill Nunn from 1969 to 1975, the Steelers relied heavily on players from HBCUs. The Steelers drafted twice the league average and more than any other team. From 1972 to 1979, with those players in their prime years, the Steelers won four Super Bowls in six seasons—a record that stands today. They have since won two more Super Bowls. Clearly, this commitment to diversity was a competitive advantage.

Bill Nunn Jr., Francis Nunn, Lynell Nunn, Bill Nunn III | Courtesy of Pittsburgh Steelers

Joe Gordon, Dan Rooney, Myron Cope | Courtesy of Pittsburgh Steelers

Bill Cowher, Dan Rooney, Chuck Noll | Courtesy of Pittsburgh Steelers

The Steel Curtain: Dwight White, Ernie Holmes, Joe Greene, L.C. Greenwood
Courtesy of Pittsburgh Steelers

Art Rooney Sr., Chuck Noll, Dan Rooney | Courtesy of Pittsburgh Steelers

George Halas and Joe Greene | Phil Sandlin/Associated Press

Joe Greene and L.C. Greenwood | Courtesy of Pittsburgh Steelers

CONCLUSION

The Steelers were a test case for everything that my father believed about how to run a successful business that had meaning beyond the bottom line. His long-range vision and design for the Steelers—and the executive team he assembled 50 years ago—laid the groundwork for the sustainable success and popularity the Steelers have had ever since. The Steelers now—a perennial playoff team with a vast international fan base—are the product of meticulous planning, deft hiring, patience and management that emphasized a feeling of community and bred a sense of trust.

STORY III | PEACEMAKER

Dan Rooney

IRELAND

STORY III | PEACEMAKER: **IRELAND**

Northern Ireland, a province of six counties that remained part of the United Kingdom after the rest of Ireland won its independence nearly a century ago, was one of the Western world's most challenging and complicated problems in the 1970s. In the United States, some Irish-Americans were encouraging armed resistance to British rule with money, weapons and political support. On the other side of Ireland's border, in the Irish Republic, the economy was stagnant and new generations of young people were looking elsewhere for jobs and a future. Double-digit unemployment seemed permanent in the Republic, while in the North, a conflict with roots going back centuries became worse with each passing year.

Our family had a heartfelt appreciation of Irish culture and history. The Rooneys were from Newry in Northern Ireland and for a good portion of his early life, my father, like many other Irish-American Catholics, tended to blame the British and Northern Ireland's majority Protestant population for the conflict known as The Troubles. But once he learned more about the conflict, the right thing to do became clear: He decided not to shout slogans from the sidelines, but to take an active role in promoting peace and prosperity for all Irish people. It required courage, because many Irish-Americans believed violence was the answer to Ireland's problems, and it surely required the long view. He had a vision of a tormented island at peace with itself and prosperous, with the help of Irish-Americans like himself.

As a philanthropist and, later, as the U.S. ambassador to Ireland, my father brought together people with opposing views—with views he himself opposed—and sought to find common ground and room for compromise by appealing to their better natures. It was hard and frustrating work, and it required an ability to remain focused on the long-term goal while working on incremental advances.

SEVEN

IRISH ROOTS

THE ROONEY IMMIGRANT STORY GOES BACK MANY DECADES, to my great-great-grandparents, who left Ireland in the 19th century at a time when millions of Irish, most of them impoverished Catholics, left their homes and families to escape hunger and oppression. Our family's story is a little unusual because it involved several trips across the Atlantic as my ancestors looked for work and a better life. The family moved from Newry to Canada, to Wales, to Ohio and finally to Pittsburgh, where my great-grandfather opened a bar and served as a district leader for the local political organization headed by the Coyne family. (A descendant of the Coynes recently won election to Congress from western Pennsylvania—Conor Lamb, a Democrat, although the Coyne machine was Republican.)

My grandfather was raised in the city's North Side, which was home to a large Irish community and where it was not uncommon to hear the Irish language spoken in the neighborhood's churches, social halls and pubs.

The immigrant experience, the feeling of being an outsider but also being very much a part of a close-knit community, was fundamental to his family and their friends. The Irish came to Pittsburgh for the same reason that other groups left behind all they knew and loved in the Old World: There was work to be had in the city's hundreds of factories, which were powered by the coal dug by other immigrants in and around Pennsylvania.

My grandfather and father both married Irish girls—my grandmother was Kathleen McNulty, and my mother, Patricia Regan, is the daughter of immigrants from County Mayo who left in the 1920s. My maternal grandfather, Martin Regan, used to tell my father stories about the old country when he was courting my mother, and he was not shy about breaking into song, which inspired my father's love of Irish music. My parents traveled to Ireland in 1971 along with Lou Spadia, who was then president of the San Francisco 49ers, and his wife, Maggie. It was a memorable occasion, because my mother met her grandmother, Mary Duffy, for the first time. She lived in a two-room thatched roof cottage in a tiny village in County Mayo. She was quite old and for a while thought Patricia, my mother, was her daughter, although eventually it was all sorted out. Mary Duffy died soon afterward, which made that visit all the more poignant for my parents.

In addition to stories, music and family connections in Ireland, though, there was politics. The endless conflict with the British over Ireland's claims to political, cultural and economic independence was a real presence on the North Side and in many other Irish neighborhoods during my father's childhood and, in fact, well into his later years. That's because of the island's century-old partition and Northern Ireland's history of anti-Catholic discrimination.

In 1921, Irish rebels had forced Britain to the bargaining table after a brief but bloody war that began just after World War I ended in late 1918. The ensuing peace treaty was a hard compromise for many Irish people: Britain divided the island, granting a form of self-government to a new, 26-county entity called the Irish Free State. But it retained control of the island's other six counties, creating a province called Northern Ireland that remained within the United Kingdom.

Many Americans never fully understood the causes of the conflict in Northern Ireland. That's because the divisions there can be traced back hundreds of years, to the beginning of a split within Christianity between the Roman Catholic Church and various Protestant sects centuries ago. It's important to understand that the majority of Ireland's population was and remains Catholic. They are descendants of the native Gaelic Irish. The island's minority Protestant population is, for the most part, descended from English and Scots settlers who have been in Ireland longer than the United States has been an independent country.

When the English King Henry VIII split with the Roman Catholic Church in the 16th century and established the Church of England, Catholics who remained loyal to the pope were regarded as potential traitors. The English already were a presence in Ireland at the time, and despite new laws that made it very difficult to remain Catholic, the Irish refused to convert to the Church of England or other forms of Protestantism. That set the stage for the religious dimension to Ireland's conflict: The island's Catholic majority saw its land taken away, its religion virtually outlawed, and its culture and language suppressed. Protestants held high political office and dominated the island's land-owning classes.

That religious divide is what led to Ireland's actual division in 1921. Protestants in the island's northeast corner wished to remain part of the United Kingdom, a notion that was anathema to Irish nationalists. But Britain demanded this concession as the price for allowing the rest of Ireland to govern its domestic affairs. And so Northern Ireland was created, with a built-in pro-British Protestant majority determined to hold onto power at the expense of Catholics, who made up a third of the population.

In the years following partition, the government of Northern Ireland treated Catholics as second-class citizens, openly discriminated against in virtually every walk of life. Good jobs in the province's factories and especially in Belfast's famous shipyards were reserved for Protestants, and Catholics had little political power, thanks to political gerrymandering of their local political districts.

The conflict wasn't really about religion—the two sides weren't debating theology. It was about power and identity. The Protestants saw themselves as British who were loyal to the Crown and the United Kingdom. They preferred the label of "loyalists" or "unionists." The Catholics saw themselves as Irish who believed that all of Ireland should be independent of Britain, and they referred to themselves as "nationalists" or "republicans"—meaning that they believed in a republic governing all 32 of Ireland's counties, not just the 26 that won independence in 1921.

Complicated enough for you? Welcome to Irish history!

The plight of Northern Ireland's Catholics was a sore point among many Irish Catholics in America, even those far removed from the immigrant experience.

In every city with a significant Irish-American population, Pittsburgh included, there were organizations that made no secret of their support for those who stockpiled arms and ammunition while they planned the next Irish rebellion.

In the 1960s, many young Catholics in Northern Ireland looked across the Atlantic and found inspiration not from the old Irish-American organizations that traditionally supported them, but from Dr. Martin Luther King Jr., the Southern Christian Leadership Conference, and the brave African-American men, women and children who were marching for their civil rights in places like Selma and Birmingham. In late October 1968, several months after Dr. King was assassinated and many U.S. cities suffered through a summer of violence, civil rights marchers in Northern Ireland were attacked and beaten by members of the province's police force, the Royal Ulster Constabulary.

British troops were soon deployed to Northern Ireland, supposedly to keep the peace between Catholic and Protestant, or nationalist and unionist, but it soon became clear that they were there to enforce Protestant supremacy. On January 30, 1972, paratroopers opened fire on a civil rights demonstration in Derry, killing 13 unarmed marchers (a 14th victim died several months later). The day became known as "Bloody Sunday." The paratroopers' commander was given one of Britain's highest honors at the end of the year, the Order of the British Empire.

Reaction was swift in coming. The Irish Republican Army had been dormant for years, but especially after the killings in Derry, a new generation of recruits began a campaign of violence against the police and soldiers, which led in turn to the formation of several Protestant militia groups that terrorized Catholic neighborhoods. Bombings and killings soon were commonplace in Northern Ireland, and it seemed as though every few weeks brought news of some fresh outrage. Three thousand people would lose their lives over the next quarter century, and Northern Ireland became known as a place where deep hatreds made compromise impossible.

Irish-Americans were outraged, and soon many were looking for a way to help the Catholics of Northern Ireland fight against state-sponsored discrimination that seemed to be enforced by Ireland's traditional enemy, the British army. A new American group called Irish Northern Aid claimed to be raising money for the families of IRA members taken prisoner, but, in fact, it was trying to get guns and funds to the IRA itself. Many Irish-Americans, including people my father knew, believed violence had to be answered with violence. One of the pubs in the neighborhood collected money in a coffee can for "the cause."

Dan Rooney felt as strongly as anyone that the system in Northern Ireland was unjust and was built on bigotry. But he also believed that peace in Ireland would never be achieved without hope and opportunity, not just in Northern Ireland but throughout the whole island. The Irish Republic and the United Kingdom had recently joined what was then called the Common Market, the precursor to today's European Union, but no great boom followed. Quite the opposite— the jobs in the shipyards and factories of Northern Ireland began to disappear, while in the Republic, double-digit unemployment, high taxes and ballooning government deficits led to anemic economic growth (less than 2 percent a year) and continued emigration of young people.

As an Irish-American who knew his history, as the grandson of Irish immigrants on his mother's side, my father had a frame of reference for the Ireland of the 1970s. He understood the anger and resentments of other Irish-Americans who had been raised on stories about Irish rebellions that began heroically and ended tragically, and he knew people who believed their families had been forced to leave their native land because of British oppression or because of the inequities that were a legacy of British rule.

But he also had another frame of reference that helped him understand Northern Ireland in ways that, frankly, many other Irish-Americans didn't share— he saw a connection between the Catholic struggle for civil rights in the North and the civil rights movement in America.

A civil rights attorney, Bill McNally, remembered that Dan saw housing as a key to achieving justice, whether in Northern Ireland or the United States. Bill recalled recently that Dan once told him that "if you have people of different backgrounds living near each other, it's a lot harder to hate each other and be afraid of each other." There's a lesson for the business world and the workplace of the 21st century: Eliminate the unknown and there's a good chance you can eliminate fear and hatred.

With that lesson in mind, Daniel Rooney sought to find a better way for the people—all of the people—of Ireland.

Tony O'Reilly, a native of Dublin, arrived in Pittsburgh in 1971 to take the helm at Heinz, the food-processing company best known for its ketchup. Hardly anybody in Pittsburgh realized it, but O'Reilly was an enormous sports legend in Ireland. He became a rugby star in 1955 at the age of 18 and went on to play for the Irish national team until 1970. He left the field as Ireland's most-celebrated rugby player ever and would eventually be enshrined in the International Rugby Hall of Fame.

He arrived in Pittsburgh with a reputation for business that matched his record on the rugby pitch. He soon became the president of Heinz, then CEO and later chairman. An ambitious businessman on his own, he bought one of Ireland's premier newspapers, the Irish Independent, and became a major shareholder in several other companies, including Waterford Wedgewood.

Dan Rooney met O'Reilly at a party not long after he arrived in Pittsburgh from Dublin. After they were introduced, O'Reilly said, "I always liked American football. I think I could play. Do you mind if I worked out with the boys?"

Dan said he was sure it could be arranged, thinking O'Reilly meant stopping by a Steelers' practice session and maybe doing some running with the team. But that's not what O'Reilly, who was 38 years old at the time, had in mind.

"I want to go out and play with the pads and run the plays," he said. That should give you an idea of the kind of person Tony O'Reilly has always been. He fancied himself a running back, and while he was fast and in good shape, well, it wasn't going to happen.

Dan suggested that he might be just a little too old to take up American football. Tony must have taken no offense, because the two of them became lifelong friends and partners in an organization that has raised more than $600 million for organizations devoted to peace, reconciliation and economic development on both sides of the border in Ireland.

You might say they were an unlikely pair. O'Reilly was and remains an outgoing, voluble personality who didn't shy away from the press. My father was a reserved and private person who was content to let others bask in the spotlight of publicity. He wasn't much for press conferences. But nobody worked the phones better than he did.

Together, O'Reilly and Dan Rooney were a formidable partnership. My mother recalled my father sharing his knowledge "about this country and our political workings" with O'Reilly through the years.

Among the many things they shared was a belief that they could not stand by while Ireland suffered, whether from violence or economic malaise. Their political and economic clout in the United States offered them an opportunity to make a difference in Ireland. And they seized that opportunity.

O'Reilly's perspective on Northern Ireland was different from the conventional wisdom in many Irish-American neighborhoods. O'Reilly was a native of Ireland and had lived through the beginnings of the Troubles. Even though he didn't live in the North, nobody in Ireland was very far from the violence. "I tried to explain to Dan, 'You have got to remember that Northern Ireland has been around for years—it was not just the British against the Catholic Irish of the North,'" O'Reilly said. "It was never that simple. Not that one side was completely right, or that one side could somehow leave. I believe he felt I had given him a good education."

He did indeed. He taught my father that the "Brits out" perspective that many Irish-Americans held was unrealistic—the Loyalists of Northern Ireland were the descendants of people who had been in Ireland longer than most families have been in the United States.

Not long after O'Reilly met Dan, he was asked to hold a gala fundraiser in New York for Dublin's Royal College of Surgeons, a wonderful institution that has trained generations of Irish medical doctors. He had held an Irish-themed charity dinner a year earlier, but it turned out to be a disaster. "We have to have a second dinner to pay for the initial dinner," he said, only half-kidding.

O'Reilly came up with the idea of honoring my grandfather at the dinner. His timing could not have been better. The dinner, held in the grand ballroom of the Waldorf Astoria Hotel in midtown Manhattan, took place right after the Steelers won Super Bowl IX in January 1975, over the Minnesota Vikings. It was the first Steelers' Super Bowl championship and the beginning of the Steel Curtain dynasty.

Dan Rooney looked out at the vast room, filled to capacity, and turned to O'Reilly. "This is really big," he said. "We've got to keep this banquet going, year after year."

The following year, in 1976, Tony and Dan announced the creation of The Ireland Funds, an organization dedicated to peace, culture and charity. It was the beginning of an organization and a cause to which Dan Rooney would be devoted for the rest of his life, and which helped bring about profound change in Ireland on both sides of the border.

At the time, though, it seemed like an almost-impossible task.

In the mid-1970s, the situation in Northern Ireland was getting worse with each passing month as a faction of the IRA called the Provisional IRA ramped up its campaign of bombing and targeted killings of police officers and British troops. Meanwhile, Loyalist paramilitaries, sometimes working in collaboration with security forces, murdered Catholics and sought to enforce the virtual segregation of Catholics from the province's civic life. Just a few weeks before Tony and Dan created The Ireland Funds, five Catholic civilians had been murdered in cold blood by a Loyalist militia group. A day later, members of the IRA stopped a bus near the location of the previous night's killings. Ten Protestants on their way to work were shot to death in retaliation. Meanwhile, Ireland's foreign minister and future prime minister, Garret FitzGerald, said that the Irish Northern Aid Committee, or Noraid, had raised as much as $2 million in the United States, with most of the money going to the IRA for guns and ammunition.

It wasn't just the British who were worried about the American connection to the IRA or its supporters in Northern Ireland. The Irish government was equally concerned, so much so that when officials with Jimmy Carter's presidential campaign came to Pittsburgh in 1976 to meet with representatives of the Irish National Caucus, a group that supported reunification of Ireland and was thought to be sympathetic to the IRA, Dublin made its displeasure known. Carter later told the Irish government that his campaign didn't realize whom they were dealing with.

Most Irish-Americans didn't pay a great deal of attention to what was happening across the Atlantic, especially in the 1970s, when the United States suffered through political scandals, oil shortages, inflation and economic stagnation. But among those who were active, most believed the IRA's campaign was necessary and they were willing to contribute their time and money in support of the cause. "They were seeing the headlines where Catholics were being burned out of their homes in Derry and Belfast by Loyalist mobs," recalled former Irish diplomat Ted Smyth. "The British government didn't seem to be doing much about it." Among the most notorious IRA supporters was the Boston gangster James "Whitey" Bulger, who raised money and sent weapons to the North, including a haul of seven tons of guns and ammunition hidden in the coffins of dead Irish immigrants whose bodies were shipped back to Ireland for burial. A member of his infamous Winter Hill gang, Patrick Nee, wrote that he saw himself as "a criminal with a passion: to drive the British out of Ireland."

Those like Rooney who spoke out for another way were often criticized publicly as collaborators with the British in oppressing Northern Ireland's Catholics. Four Irish-American politicians came in for particular abuse: Senator Edward Kennedy and House Speaker Tip O'Neill of Massachusetts and Senator Daniel Patrick Moynihan and Governor Hugh Carey of New York. They began to speak out against the IRA just as O'Reilly and Rooney were launching The Ireland Funds, and together they created an alliance that showed the world that those who advocated for and financed violence in Northern Ireland did not speak for all of Irish America.

They issued a statement on St. Patrick's Day, 1977, urging Irish-Americans to "renounce any action that promotes the current violence or provides support or encouragement for organizations engaged in violence." A few weeks later, Carey went to Ireland to speak at the College of Surgeons, the very institution for which Rooney and O'Reilly had raised money at the dinner honoring my grandfather. He used the occasion to denounce "the apostles of death and violence."

To give you a sense of how polarized the debate over Northern Ireland was, Carey's remarks were bitterly condemned in his home state of New York, where Noraid was based. A prominent attorney aligned with Noraid described Carey's speech as a "betrayal." Later that year, pro-IRA demonstrators picketed outside a New York Democratic Party dinner because Carey was the event's honoree.

Dan and Tony invited Ted Kennedy to address The Ireland Funds gala in 1977. Once again, the ballroom in the Waldorf was packed, but this time the mood was less celebratory than when my grandfather was the main honoree and everybody wanted to talk about the Steelers and their Super Bowl title. Kennedy spoke less than a month after Carey's speech in Dublin, and he used part of his talk to deliver the same message the governor delivered. "While the killing in Northern Ireland goes on, let no American have it on his conscience that his efforts or his dollars helped to make the violence worse," Kennedy said.

There was another featured speaker that night, although he was not nearly as well-known as Kennedy. His name was John Hume, a Catholic, a native of Derry and a member of the Social Democratic and Labour Party in Northern Ireland. He led civil rights marches in the North in the late 1960s and was elected to Northern Ireland's provincial legislature in 1973. By 1977, he had emerged as a moral force for nonviolence and social justice in the North, a position that earned him the contempt of IRA supporters on both sides of the Atlantic. Hume saw Irish-Americans as potential allies in his emerging campaign to use ballots, not bullets, to achieve social and political change.

He told the crowd at the Waldorf that despite all the criticism leveled at Moynihan, Carey, Kennedy and O'Neill, their condemnation of violence and the supporters of violence in America was well-received in Ireland. Their sentiments, he said, spoke for "the vast mass of the people of Ireland."

Hume's words, his sincerity and his passionate belief in the power of nonviolence made a deep impression on Dan. His appearance at The Ireland Funds dinner in 1977 marked the beginning of my father's decades-long friendship with one of the truly great Irishmen of our time, or any time for that matter. John Hume was the Irish Gandhi during the Troubles. He never wavered in his belief that the moral force of his argument would win out over those who believed that violence was the only answer to Ireland's injustices.

John Hume would go on to become a co-recipient of the Nobel Peace Prize in 1998 for his role in helping to end the conflict in Northern Ireland. But on that night at the Waldorf in 1977, peace and peace prizes seemed almost impossible to imagine.

The Irish journalist Maurice Fitzpatrick observed that the organization Daniel Rooney and Tony O'Reilly founded was "the antithesis of the IRA" because it "focused on reconciliation and working with Hume." Rooney, O'Reilly and a third founding partner, Chuck Daly, a native of Ireland and a former U.S. Marine, "tried to get away from the view that the evil English were persecuting the woebegone Catholics in the North." What's more, Fitzpatrick noted, the fund also sought "to give perspective to the Protestant side of the story."

And that, in keeping with Dan's overall philosophy, was the right thing to do. The situation in Northern Ireland was complicated. The views of the province's Protestant majority, which saw itself as British, had to be recognized. Dan Rooney's business background helped him here, because he was not burdened with the weight of outdated political dogma and ideologies. He was interested in pragmatic problem-solving, and it was clear to him, and others, that no problems would be solved in Ireland by simply pretending that there was only one point of view in the conflict there.

As The Ireland Funds grew through the late 1970s and into the 1980s, it became known for doing the right thing by all communities in the North as well as in the Irish Republic. Dan recalled that attendees at the Funds' earliest galas urged him to expand the list of beneficiaries and the pool of donors. "Soon we found that those who loved Ireland were willing to make contributions to [other] worthy charities," he said.

Those worthy charities included a workshop in Belfast, where people who were badly wounded by the violence in the North learned crafts to help them become more self-sufficient despite a variety of disabilities; a suicide prevention service; and a program that researched and promoted human rights. Another charity served as an example of the kind of long-term good the Funds sought to achieve: a group called the Corrymeela Community, which was (and still is) a retreat center in County Antrim outside Belfast. It was a place where Catholics and Protestants came together to talk about all of the issues that divided them, from mixed marriages (they were rare, but in the 1970s they could rip apart families) to the deaths of loved ones, many of them innocent victims, killed in the fighting. The community was founded in 1965, before the violence in the North became a virtual war, by a former chaplain in World War II named Ray Davey. The community still exists and plays host to about 11,000 people a year as the province and its people still recover from generations of turmoil and injustice.

The Funds' annual gala became not just a charity dinner but a networking event for Irish causes as well as something like a political convention, which isn't surprising given Irish-American success in politics. Tip O'Neill gave the keynote speech in 1978, not long after he began his decade-long reign as speaker of the House, and his star power plus the Fund's growing reputation helped raise more than $400,000 in a single night—and that was in 1978 money.

The Funds' generosity extended to the entire island of Ireland, not just the province of Northern Ireland. Dan Rooney was determined to give the Irish Republic whatever help he could in developing a more modern economy. Part of Ireland's charm is the large portions of the country that remained rural and agricultural—but the charm often hid poverty, some of it generational. Ireland continued to lose people, especially from the less-developed parts of the island, because they saw no opportunity in a country that was among the poorest in Western Europe. From 1975 to 1980, the long-term unemployment rate in the Irish Republic rose from about 20 percent to almost 35 percent, foreshadowing another period of mass migration of young people, many of whom came to the United States without papers in hopes of finding work through Irish-American networks.

Through Dan's direction, The Ireland Funds began to focus on providing seed money for U.S. investment in the Irish Republic. Loretta Brennan Glucksman, a philanthropist and patron of the arts well-known on both sides of the Atlantic, recalled that the Funds' "bottom line was towards investment, almost regardless of what sector it would land, and Dan particularly understood these facts."

My father's relationship with other American business leaders allowed him to talk up the advantages of investing in Ireland and of promoting peace. Smyth, the former Irish diplomat, said Dan's standing as a "rock star in Irish America" gave him credibility and standing with other Irish-American business leaders. So they listened when he explained, without resorting to sentiment or blarney, that there were opportunities in Ireland. The country had a young, highly skilled work force, and because the Industrial Revolution pretty much passed over Ireland save for Belfast and a few other pockets, there was no aging infrastructure and almost literally no old ways of doing business to hamper an entrepreneur's wish to create jobs, products and services designed for the late 20th and early 21st centuries. Ted Smyth said that Dan "helped to change the mindset that many had about doing business in Ireland."

Some of the Funds' money went to programs at Irish universities, including Trinity College, University College Galway, Limerick University and University College Dublin, to incubate high-tech jobs and research. Funds also went to support Ireland's Integrated Education Fund, which supported the religious integration of the Irish school system, which was and for the most part remains controlled by the Catholic Church.

As the work grew, additional chapters were formed and dinners held in cities beyond New York. Irish-American business leaders clamored to be part of what was becoming an exemplary charitable organization that sought to bring peace and prosperity to an island that knew too little of each.

This was all quite wonderful, although once again, my father had to wrestle with his natural discomfort with these overt displays of wealth and the focus on money. He knew it was all for a good cause, but still: The lavish ballrooms, the expensive meals, the well-dressed crowds were not his style. He surely would have preferred to raise as much money as possible through a solicitation by mail, or with a phone call. But he knew that simply wasn't possible. So he gritted his teeth, put on his tuxedo and did what he could to bring healing to Ireland.

Sometimes, though, things were not so peaceful within the organization itself, and there my father played a role similar to the one he played as a mediator when the NFL's owners couldn't come to an agreement on important labor and revenue issues.

At some point in the Funds' formative years, Tony O'Reilly and Chuck Daly, the ex-Marine and former aide to John F. Kennedy who became a critical partner in the Funds' endeavors, were at odds over the relative merits of two Irish-American politicians who shall remain anonymous. Things got so out of hand that O'Reilly shouted at Daly, "You don't have to remain on this board!"

"You're goddamn right I don't," Daly shot back before turning on his heel and leaving a meeting of the Funds' board.

Everybody figured that was the last they'd ever hear from Chuck Daly. But a week later, Dan called him—he hadn't been able to attend the meeting where the fireworks went off. But he heard all about it.

He spoke softly. He told Daly that he had spoken with Tony and that Tony didn't want him to leave. "And you shouldn't want to get off this board," Dan said, appealing to Daly's better angels.

"He just quietly put it back together," Daly recalled years later.

The late 1970s and early 1980s brought the world's attention to Northern Ireland, and not for good reasons. The charitable work of The Ireland Funds no doubt was making an impact, slowly but surely, but it seemed as if nothing could bring all sides together in that small corner of the globe.

In late August 1979, one of World War II's great heroes, Lord Louis Mountbatten, was killed when a radio-controlled bomb hidden somewhere on his fishing boat exploded. Mountbatten, a member of Britain's Royal Family, had invited several family members to join him for a day of fishing aboard his 30-foot boat off the Irish coast. The blast killed Mountbatten and three others, including two children.

An IRA man had planted the bomb. Mountbatten's murder shocked many Irish-Americans, my parents included, because they remembered him for the role he played in defeating the Axis. "It was quite sad because being in America, you were familiar with Lord Mountbatten because of World War II," my mother recalled. "It was a very sad time." But my father didn't give in to despair. "That didn't slow down [my father] one bit. It more or less gave him more energy," my mother said.

A new British prime minister, Margaret Thatcher, was determined to crush the IRA once and for all. The IRA and its sympathizers were looking to provoke a confrontation with her, and they found a cause in early 1981: Imprisoned members of the IRA and another group, the Irish National Liberation Army, demanded to be treated as prisoners of war, rather than common criminals. Among other things, they wanted to wear civilian clothes rather than prison uniforms. The Thatcher government refused, as previous governments had, and on March 1, 1981, a 27-year-old IRA prisoner named Bobby Sands began a hunger strike. Then, according to plan, another prisoner went on a hunger strike, and then another. The idea was to enhance the spectacle of individual prisoners taking on the power of the British government.

Incredibly, Sands was elected to the House of Commons while on hunger strike, a sign that public opinion was shifting. Many thought Thatcher would back down rather than risk seeing an elected member of Parliament starve himself to death over what seemed to be little more than a symbolic issue. But Thatcher refused any concessions, famously saying, "Crime is crime is crime, it is not political." Sands died on May 5 after 66 days without food.

The Ireland Funds held a fundraiser at the Waldorf not long after Sands' death. The situation was tense, both outside and inside the hotel, as IRA sympathizers were picketing near the hotel's entrance. Dan Rooney, dressed in black tie, chose not to ignore the protesters but went to their picket line and spoke with a few. They rejected his approach of reconciliation, blaming people like him as well as the British for continued injustice in Ireland. Unlike them, however, Dan was willing to hear another point of view and to consider the thoughts of those who disagreed with him. That was very much his method of operation, no matter what the setting. He respected those on the other side of a debate or the bargaining table, and he understood that they deserved an opportunity to present their point of view. That doesn't mean he simply acceded to their demands or pretended to agree with them for the sake of keeping peace. Instead he believed it was possible to respect another's point of view while still retaining his own core principles and beliefs. And, he found, sometimes the respect he showed others led to respect for his point of view as well.

Later that night, as a band was playing music between speeches, a nun wandered up to a microphone, grabbed hold of it and began denouncing the British. The shocked bandleader had his musicians play louder, but that didn't work—the nun began screaming. Chuck Daly leaped from his seat, asked the band to stop playing and spoke quietly with the nun. "Sister," he said, "no one in this hall wants to hurt you. I know how you feel. I'll ask the band to stay quiet if you agree to say only a few more words."

"Promise?" the nun asked.

Daly nodded.

The nun read from some notes for about two minutes and then left.

My father later said that he felt like crying that night.

Nine other hunger strikers died, one by one, through the spring and summer, as the world looked on. The strike was called off in October, but its effects lingered for years. It further polarized the two sides in Northern Ireland, created a new set of heroes for one group and villains for another. Sixty-one people, including 34 civilians, were killed by one side or the other during the hunger strikes. And in October 1984, the IRA tried to exact revenge on Thatcher by planting a bomb in a hotel in which she was staying during a Conservative Party conference in Brighton, England. Five people died, but Thatcher escaped. The IRA immediately issued a chilling statement directed at the prime minister: "Today we were unlucky, but remember we only have to be lucky once. You will have to be lucky always."

Ten years after Dan Rooney and Tony O'Reilly created The Ireland Funds, it was all too evident that the need for its three-fold mission of peace, culture and charity had only grown more urgent. More than 2,000 people had lost their lives—soldiers, police and civilians alike—by the mid-1980s, and there was no end in sight. But thanks to the work of the Fund and of Irish-American leaders like O'Neill, Kennedy, Carey and Moynihan, it was clear that groups like Noraid spoke for only a small, although loud, portion of Irish America.

The Funds was not the only prominent Irish-American organization seeking to establish better understanding and cooperation on both sides of the Atlantic. The American Irish Foundation had been created in the summer of 1963 by two

American-born presidents, John F. Kennedy of the United States and New York native Eamon de Valera, the president of Ireland. It did wonderful work, but it did present a bit of a problem for Dan. Many people confused the Funds with the Foundation, and vice versa. Rooney suggested that it might help the cause better if the two became one. The idea was put on the table at a meeting in the Waldorf in 1986 and it received something less than unanimous agreement. Again, it seemed as though some people, for perfectly good reasons, were looking only at the short term—how this merger would affect them or their particular interest. Dan Rooney was more interested in the long game: He believed one large centralized organization would do more good for more people than two smaller groups competing with each other for funds and attention.

His argument prevailed, and on March 17, 1987—St. Patrick's Day—Dan Rooney and his colleagues were at the White House as President Ronald Reagan announced the creation of a new, merged organization called the American Ireland Fund. During the ceremony, the president praised the leaders of the organization, my father included. "George Bernard Shaw once wrote: 'The worst sin towards our fellow creatures is not to hate them, but to be indifferent to them. That's the essence of inhumanity.' Well, no one involved here could ever be labeled indifferent. With us today are William Vincent, Daniel Rooney and John Brogan. … And God bless the fine work that is being done. This type of commitment … is a part of the American way of life, perhaps a part that can be traced back to Ireland."

Not long thereafter, Dan and his colleagues named a new chairman for the Fund, Loretta Brennan Glucksman, who revitalized the board and expanded its reach.

The new energy could not have come at a better time, because in Ireland, the mists of history were about to give way to a hopeful dawn.

EIGHT

THE COMING OF PEACE

TONY O'REILLY ONCE SAID THAT HE SAW DAN'S VIEWS ON NORTHERN IRELAND EVOLVE as he became better informed about the conflict there. O'Reilly noted that the traditional Irish-American view of the conflict tended to ignore the presence of a million Protestants in Northern Ireland, many of whom treasured the province's connection to Britain. Perhaps it took a native-born Irishman to emphasize that point to an Irish-American like Dan Rooney.

But then again, because my father was born in the United States, and because he was a businessman, he brought a unique perspective to the conflict in the North that helped other Americans, especially business leaders, understand the Troubles through an American lens.

He came to see the conflict not as one rooted in theological differences or in medieval history, but as a matter of civil rights and denied opportunity. That would have sounded familiar to Americans of goodwill, because they were living through a similar struggle in the United States at the time.

In 1982, three years after the IRA killed Lord Mountbatten and a year after the 10 hunger strikers starved to death, Dan contacted Bill McNally, the civil rights lawyer. He was running an organization that provided legal assistance to poor, mostly minority, defendants in the Boston area. McNally began his career in Chicago in 1968, when protesters and police battled each other on the city's streets during the Democratic National Convention. McNally represented Bobby Seale, the African-American activist and founder of the Black Panthers, who was tried for conspiracy and incitement to riot after the convention along with co-defendants Abbie Hoffman, Jerry Rubin, Tom Hayden and four others.

Dan wanted McNally to come to work for the American Ireland Fund, and asked him to come by for an interview. Why in the world, McNally wondered, would he want to take a job involving Ireland and Northern Ireland, issues he knew nothing about and seemed happy to keep that way?

Dan saw what McNally and so many other Americans did not: The issue in Northern Ireland and the issues McNally worked on in Chicago and Boston were the same.

"Let me tell you something," he told McNally during that interview. "You go to Belfast, and you walk around, and you come back and tell me if it isn't identical to the American civil rights situation. You just change the words 'black' and 'white' to 'Protestant' and 'Catholic.' The issues are the same—they're jobs and housing and voting."

Years later, McNally recalled my father speaking in a "quiet, calm" demeanor as he explained why working for the Fund was a natural for somebody with his interests in civil rights and social justice.

"And he was dead right about that," McNally said.

The violence in Northern Ireland captured the headlines in the 1980s and into the 1990s, but the underlying conditions that Catholics faced on a daily basis—discrimination in housing and employment, a lack of opportunity and a general sense of hopelessness—received less attention. Dan—because of his experience as an American who lived through the civil rights era, as a business leader who employed a large number of African-Americans, and as a sports executive who sought to recruit the best talent available regardless of race—understood that jobs, justice and opportunity were key to winning peace in the north.

It was a view he shared with John Hume.

As the leader of Northern Ireland's Social Democratic and Labour Party, Hume was a voice against the violence of the IRA and the injustice that was built into the very existence of the province. Dan saw Hume as not just a politician, but a moral leader.

My parents became regular visitors to Northern Ireland in the 1970s and often visited Hume and his wife and family in their home in the Bogside section of Derry, a predominantly Catholic neighborhood. Belfast was quickly becoming noted as the Beirut of Ireland, but Derry was a dangerous place as well. We often joked to our parents about their frequent "vacations" to visit the Humes. Other families from western Pennsylvania vacationed in California or Florida, we said, but our parents went to Northern Ireland at a time when soldiers patrolled the streets in full battle gear.

Of course, these trips weren't meant for sightseeing, although there are plenty of sights worth seeing in Northern Ireland. Dan was not only strengthening a bond with a true peacemaker but also was witnessing with his own eyes some of the positive change the American Ireland Fund was making in the North, and how much still needed to be done.

Patricia Hume, the wife of John Hume, described what it was like in Derry during those years. "There were riots on the street every single day," she said. "Every single day there were bombs going off. …There were very few shops. There were very few factories. The place was like a dead town. It was just a dead-end place. That's how awful life was."

It was similarly grim in the place my ancestors called home until they left in search of a better life. Newry, a town of about 26,000 in the southern part of Northern Ireland, had the appearance of a military encampment because of its proximity to the border with the Irish Republic. British troops and fully militarized police officers were a constant presence, and so was the IRA. "Unemployment was over 30 percent," recalled Seamus Mallon, who represented the area in the British Parliament. "Young people had no prospects and the ongoing IRA violence and counterviolence by the British was ruining the lives of so many people and yet was attractive to people with no hopes for the future. There was an air of despondency."

The violence and dismal economic prospects affected one neighborhood in particular, Mallon said. The locals called it "Rooney's Meadow," named, perhaps, for distant and long-gone relatives.

But amid the despair, there was hope, too, thanks to the tenacious spirit of Northern Ireland's residents, Protestant and Catholic alike, and also thanks to several projects the American Ireland Fund supported. The Apex Housing Association was founded in Derry in the 1960s to raise funds to improve the city's dilapidated housing stock and to encourage home ownership. Later, the Fund helped the Learmount Community Development Corp. provide training and other assistance to Derry residents from all communities. Dan took a particular interest in the funding of The Playhouse, an arts and cultural organization that sought to heal old wounds through theater, education and conversation.

As my father developed a friendship with Mallon, he introduced him to American politicians from Ted Kennedy to Tip O'Neill to Bill Clinton. He also strengthened his connection with Newry and the people in Rooney's Meadow, helping to fund a community center designed to counsel and encourage the town's young people. He also brought with him Sister Michele O'Leary, the daughter of an Irish immigrant and co-founder of the Ireland Institute of Pittsburgh. She was a member of the Sisters of Mercy, and was not exactly the shy and retiring type. Sister Michele got things done, and heaven forbid if you were an obstacle in her path. Her judgment was not always perfect: While working at St. Regis elementary school in western Pennsylvania, she spotted a student who was in no hurry to return to class after recess. "Mr. Marino," she thundered, "you need to get back to math class. You'll never make a living throwing a football around." Wisely, Dan Marino returned to math class, but he did manage to defy Sister Michele's prediction, going on to be a star quarterback at Pitt and a Hall of Famer with the Miami Dolphins.

Sister Michele and Dan shared a belief in the power of education, and they put together a program that brought college students in Newry to Pittsburgh, where they were placed in jobs with the Steelers or other local organizations and studied at one of the Pittsburgh-area partner universities. The program was originally a year, but was expanded to two years because of its success and popularity.

"They brought back with them a type of cultural drive for a community that had been lost during troubles here," Mallon said. "Those young people benefited enormously from experience—they brought new skills to places of employment and their approach to business."

Mallon and Hume never gave up during those dark years in Northern Ireland, and Dan Rooney did what he could to support them as individuals and, more generally, to help imagine a better future for the province and the entire island of Ireland. With each visit to Derry, my father's admiration for Hume and his family grew. And he made quite an impression on the Humes, particularly their children. When he visited, he always came supplied with Steelers T-shirts and a couple of footballs for the young Humes. "Our kids thought he was the coolest man on earth," Patricia Hume said.

It has been a generation since the violence in Northern Ireland came to an end. Looking back at how bad things were in the 1980s and early 1990s, it truly is miraculous to see what has taken place. So much of that change is due to John Hume, who now, in his early 80s, suffers from acute dementia and quite literally cannot recall the bad old days. His friends, allies and family agree, though, that he was always mindful of the support he received from Irish-American leaders in politics and business. As Mallon put it, Hume turned to Irish America not because he sought to curry favor with famous American leaders or wanted to enjoy their hospitality. He simply had no choice: Britain showed no signs of challenging injustice in Northern Ireland despite the Irish government's protests. America, he decided, had the power to change the dynamic.

Under his leadership, several competing political parties in the Irish Republic joined Hume's SDLP for a series of conferences called The New Ireland Forum, which envisioned a day when the border would be erased and a united Ireland, liberated of old grievances, would emerge, prosperous and peaceful. The parties delivered a thoughtful report outlining three scenarios: a united Ireland; a federated Ireland in which the North would retain some form of autonomy within the Irish Republic; or a Northern Ireland under joint rule by Britain and the Irish Republic.

British Prime Minister Margaret Thatcher's reaction was immediate: "That is out," she said.

Nevertheless, thanks in part to American political pressure, Thatcher signed an agreement in 1985 that gave the Irish Republic an advisory role in some areas of Northern Ireland policymaking, but affirmed that a united Ireland would be achieved only if a majority in the North supported such a change. The Anglo-Irish Agreement was a landmark because it signaled a place for he Irish Republic in the governance of Northern Ireland.

Dan's role in all of this was pretty simple and straightforward. He was not in the rooms where these negotiations were taking place. He wasn't given to public pronouncements designed to please a crowd. He represented no political constituencies. But he believed he had a critical role to play all the same, and that role was to work behind the scenes to encourage investment and healing, and to bring hope to the entire island of Ireland. And he used his connections and the credibility he had as an executive to mix and match politicians of goodwill with other business leaders on this side of the Atlantic so that prosperity might become the guardian of peace.

John Hume knew that thanks to Dan and others, he had the unqualified support of the Irish-American political and business community. And that added to the already formidable power of his character and moral clarity.

In 1988, Hume proposed a series of secret talks with Gerry Adams, the leader of the Sinn Fein party, which was the political arm of the IRA. For Hume and his supporters in America, including Dan Rooney, it was an incredibly dangerous moment. Adams was a global pariah—he was barred from visiting the United States because of his association with the IRA. In football terms, the proposed talks between Hume and Adams were nothing less than a Hail Mary pass, something born of sheer desperation. And any football fan knows how often a Hail Mary pass actually finds its way into the hands of a receiver.

Thousands of miles away, Dan Rooney continued to play his role as a facilitator and intermediary. Through the American Ireland Fund, in which he and Tony O'Reilly continued to play a major role, millions of philanthropic dollars poured into Ireland on both sides of the border, fostering grass-roots organizations that sought to heal old wounds as well as small businesses and start-ups that sought to create a more prosperous Ireland in all 32 counties. The Fund's galas in multiple cities across the country became a critical gathering spot for Americans in business and in politics who saw promise rather than despair in Ireland.

"He understood the barriers," Loretta Brennan Glucksman, who led the American Ireland Fund for 18 years, said of Dan, "and he approached people with that same clarity of purpose that he always had because he knew what was the right thing to do. His job was to convince others to see and to have them agree," she continued. "He had that moral certainty. …He was just so valuable because of his certainty of what was right, and the fact that he shared it with us."

Various pieces began to fall into place as all parties in Northern Ireland moved ever closer to full-fledged peace talks, even though violence continued unabated. Margaret Thatcher's successor, John Major, and Irish Prime Minister Albert Reynolds issued a statement in which both the British and Irish governments accepted the principle of self-determination in Northern Ireland. This was yet another breakthrough, because the British conceded the possibility of a united Ireland if that's what the people of Northern Ireland wanted.

In January 1994, President Bill Clinton defied his own State Department and years of precedent by granting a temporary visa to Gerry Adams, allowing him to come to New York for a conference at the Waldorf Astoria. The U.S. government routinely barred members of Sinn Fein from coming across the Atlantic to speak—and raise money—but in this case, Clinton believed the time was right. But the British were vehemently opposed, and so were many members of Clinton's Cabinet. On the other hand, influential Irish-American politicians lobbied the White House on Adams' behalf, for they sensed that change was coming in Ireland. In the end, Clinton decided to give Adams a chance.

My father opposed the Adams visa, as did many of his colleagues involved with the American Ireland Fund. Adams stood for everything Rooney and the Fund had opposed for a generation. Dan was a Hume man—he believed, as Hume did, that violence led only to more and deeper hatred. Economic development, education and justice, he believed, were the keys to bringing about social and political change in the North. There were too many Irish-Americans who saw Adams as a kind of romantic radical, and most of them had never walked the devastated streets of Derry, as my parents had. "Gerry was pretty bombastic and sure of himself," my mother recalled, and he seemed to pose a threat to everything my father had been trying to do since the mid-1970s.

It was Tony O'Reilly, though no fan of Adams, who brought Dan around on the visa issue. He persuaded him that Bill Clinton was actually employing the methods of communication and trust-building that had been hallmarks of the Fund and of their own personal style for years. O'Reilly was right, as Dan came to see. The next few years were rocky indeed, but in the end, Gerry Adams led Sinn Fein, and thus the IRA, into a historic peace process that so many, Dan included, probably never thought they'd see. In the end, President Clinton's decision to bring Adams into the peace process proved to be the right one. From that point forward, Rooney became a vocal advocate for the Clintons' work in Ireland.

The IRA announced a cease-fire in late August 1994, releasing a statement in which it said: "We believe that an opportunity to secure a just and lasting settlement has been created." A few weeks later, Loyalist paramilitaries announced that they, too, would abide by a cease-fire and allow politics and diplomacy to sort out Northern Ireland's future. As old and bitter adversaries attempted to put the past behind them, it was clear there would be a need for a neutral observer—not quite a referee, since a ref is empowered to enforce the rules of the game and penalize those who violate them, but somebody who could mediate without giving offense, prod without being tainted by accusations of bias. President Clinton, who made Northern Ireland a priority of his foreign policy, named George Mitchell, the onetime majority leader of the U.S. Senate, to be that prodding voice at the table. Mitchell's official title was "special advisor to the president and the secretary of state on economic initiatives in Ireland." In reality, he was the Clinton administration's special envoy to the Northern Ireland peace talks, the man who would try to bring together factions that had sought to kill each other for years. Now, with America's help, they would try to resolve their differences through politics, not violence.

Mitchell, a native of Maine whose mother was an immigrant from Lebanon, didn't have any connection to prominent Irish-Americans—any such connections would have roused the suspicions of Northern Ireland's Protestants, many of whom considered any Irish-American to be pro-IRA. But Dan knew him through their mutual connection with Paul Tagliabue, who succeeded Pete Rozelle as NFL commissioner, and he was delighted that Mitchell would be at the negotiating table. Like many Irish-Americans, Dan Rooney sometimes could hardly believe what he was seeing: the leaders of armed paramilitary groups, each nursing ancient grievances, sitting across from each other with the blessing of the British and Irish governments, negotiating under the watchful eye of an American politician.

My father understood that he was witnessing history in the making in Ireland. And for once, it seemed as though it could have a happy ending.

Getting there wasn't easy. The IRA broke its cease-fire in early 1996, about two months after Bill and Hillary Clinton made a spectacularly successful visit to Northern Ireland to show their support for the peace process. Sinn Fein was locked out of the talks after the IRA exploded a huge bomb in London, killing two people. But the dynamic changed again when voters in the U.K. elected a Labour government led by Tony Blair on May 1, 1997. The IRA returned to a cease-fire several weeks later, and Sinn Fein was brought back into the talks.

After months of negotiations that were often touch and go, George Mitchell announced on April 10, 1998—Good Friday—that the Irish and British governments and the several political parties in Northern Ireland had approved an agreement, the first of its kind, calling for power sharing between Protestants and Catholics, a new provincial Assembly, new institutions that offered Dublin a voice in Northern Ireland's civil society and reform of the Protestant-dominated police force. The Republic of Ireland offered to repeal a clause in its constitution claiming sovereignty over the whole island of Ireland, subject to voters' approval. The British acknowledged, for the first time, that a substantial portion of Northern Ireland's population, and a majority of the island's total population, wanted a united Ireland. The British conceded such a possibility if a majority of Northern Ireland's population supported such a goal.

The document became known as the Good Friday Agreement, and it won overwhelming approval in both the Republic of Ireland and in Northern Ireland. And in 1998, John Hume and Unionist leader David Trimble were awarded the Nobel Peace Prize. For Hume, it was the culmination of a career spent in defiance of history and expectations. The brilliance of his moral clarity had, at last, cut through the dreary mists of Northern Ireland's status quo.

The peace process in Northern Ireland was, and indeed remains, a process. But, as Patricia Hume noted, people are now living for Ireland rather than dying for Ireland. And that certainly is progress.

Dan Rooney remained an active supporter of the extraordinary reconciliation that unfolded in the North through the 1990s and into the 21st century. Sometime later, Bill Clinton took note of my father's role in building bridges in the decades before the peace process. So much of what took place in the 1990s, Clinton said, "would not have been possible without what he [Dan Rooney] did for 15 or 20 years before the so-called process started." Whether through his role with the American Ireland Fund or as private mediator, somebody who had earned a reputation as a listener with a clear moral compass, he was part of the conversations taking place on both sides of the Atlantic as leaders in Britain, Ireland and the United States sought to replace grievance with optimism.

"I'm now convinced, although I wasn't at the time, that the British government would never have involved itself in the creation of the Good Friday Agreement had it not been for the pressure from the United States, and the way in which Dan and people like him patiently broke down the State Department's opposition," said Seamus Mallon. "It's something we're all thankful for, because had it not been for that pressure, there would not have been a Good Friday Agreement and there would not have been the peace that's now been created."

In the spring of 2007, as life had returned to the streets and lanes of Northern Ireland, a new power arrangement took hold in the province. The new first minister of Northern Ireland's provincial government would be the voice of hard-line Protestant supremacy in the North, the Reverend Ian Paisley, who gained fame in the 1960s for his vitriolic anti-Catholic sermons. Serving alongside Paisley as the deputy first minister was Martin McGuinness, a onetime member of the IRA who was now a top official in Sinn Fein. He stood for everything Paisley opposed, and vice versa. But in the spirit of the Good Friday Agreement, they were now expected to share power and to settle their differences through politics and deal-making, not through bullets and incendiary rhetoric.

The two men had never had a conversation—not even about the weather, McGuinness would later joke. And if you can't talk about the weather in Ireland, well, that's a bad sign.

Dan Rooney and his colleagues at the American Ireland Fund understood how fragile and fraught the Paisley-McGuinness relationship could be. If they couldn't get along—and there was nothing about their history to inspire optimism—the peace process could easily unravel.

Dan made some calls, had several discreet conversations, and in early December 2007, Paisley and McGuinness flew to America to spend a week speaking with, and listening to, business leaders and politicians—including President George W. Bush. Arrangements were made for the two of them to ring the opening bell at the New York Stock Exchange and to share a breakfast of scrambled eggs with the city's financial elites. They were the guests of honor at a luncheon sponsored by the American Ireland Fund. Later that night, they were invited to a small reception in the home of Loretta Brennan Glucksman, the Fund's longtime chairman. "Dan wasn't there," Loretta recalled, "but he was very involved in the planning of it and in actually getting Ian and Martin to agree to come out."

Loretta had assembled about a hundred guests to meet this Northern Irish odd couple. One of those guests was actor Liam Neeson, who grew up in Northern Ireland near Paisley's church. The two found themselves seated together in a small library in Loretta's apartment, and Neeson turned to Paisley and said, "You're the reason I'm an actor." This, as you can imagine, was quite a revelation, and Paisley couldn't hide his delight. "I used to sneak into your church," Neeson told him, "and I'd listen to you and try to project my voice the way you did. And I still think that I would never have gotten into acting if it hadn't been for you."

It was turning out to be a remarkable day. Later that evening, Paisley, a large man with the booming voice that inspired a young Liam Neeson, addressed the crowd Loretta had gathered. McGuinness was in the back of the room, watching.

"I am a man preparing to meet my God," the 81-year-old Paisley said. "And I am a man of God. And I want to make sure that the work I present to him is honorable. And the fact that I am here with my respected colleague, Martin McGuinness, tonight assures me that my work has been good."

Men and women were weeping in Loretta's apartment that night. And for once, the tears shed for Northern Ireland were tears of hope and joy.

"That doesn't happen without Dan Rooney," Loretta said.

NINE

OUR MAN IN DUBLIN

IN ORDER TO BE AN EFFECTIVE MEDIATOR, whether the topic is labor relations, peace negotiations or a business transaction, it's important that all parties see you as objective and fair. The minute you take sides, you lose credibility with the other side.

Dan's quiet effectiveness on Irish issues was tied to the perception and the reality that he was willing to listen to all sides, and that while he had his own opinions, he was not a partisan and had no personal agenda other than a determination to do what he could to help bridge the divide in the homeland of his ancestors.

His approach continued to reap rewards, on and off the gridiron. The Steelers won Super Bowl XLIII in 2009, defeating the Arizona Cardinals 27-23 in one of the most exciting championship games in NFL history. The Cardinals went ahead 23-20 with just over two minutes remaining, but the Steelers regrouped, and with 35 seconds left, Santonio Holmes made the catch that was essentially the most significant in NFL history (sorry, Franco, Dwight Clark and David Tyree) to give the Steelers the win. Holmes caught nine passes that day and was named the game's MVP, which meant, of course, that he was going to Disney World.

Six weeks later, Dan Rooney found out he was also going somewhere too.

He was heading to Ireland, as America's next ambassador.

President Barack Obama nominated Daniel M. Rooney for the post on March 17, 2009 — St. Patrick's Day. "He will be an outstanding representative," Obama said. "Dan is a great friend. He and his family are as gracious and thoughtful a group of people as I know, and so I know that he is just going to do an outstanding job. And the people of Ireland, I think, will benefit greatly from him representing the United States there."

His appointment was subject to approval from the U.S. Senate, so he was summoned to appear before the Foreign Relations Committee later that spring. This was an entirely new experience for him—at the age of 76—and he understood that he'd need to prep for his date with the Senate. He was due to appear before several members of the Foreign Relations Committee on June 24. He had been carefully briefed by State Department staffer Zia Syed and was prepared for most of the anticipated questions. But a completely unscripted conversation in an elevator minutes before the hearing inspired Dan to go out on a limb during his testimony by making a promise to do something no other U.S. ambassador to Ireland had ever done.

It started with some teasing banter between my father and another nominee who was due before the Foreign Relations Committee the same day. Capricia Penavic Marshall had served as President Bill Clinton's social secretary and was nominated to become the chief protocol officer, with the rank of ambassador, under President Obama. Marshall and Rooney were scheduled to testify simultaneously, so they shared an elevator to the hearing room. She was from Cleveland and was a huge fan of the Browns, which led the future ambassador to throw a few barbs her way, to the delight of Assistant Secretary of State Richard Verma, a native of western Pennsylvania who was escorting them to the hearing room.

As the elevator neared its destination, Dan turned to Verma and repeated a concern he had voiced earlier, during the pre-hearing briefings. "I still think these guys [the senators] would like to hear of one milestone initiative for my ambassadorship," he said. Marshall jumped into the conversation, suggesting that he promise to visit every one of Ireland's 32 counties.

No U.S. ambassador to Ireland had ever done that, and for good reason—not all of Ireland's 32 counties are in the same country. The six counties that make up Northern Ireland were within the jurisdiction of the U.S. ambassador to the Court of St. James (the official title of the ambassador to Britain), so crossing the border on official business would be a breach of protocol. It wouldn't be unprecedented but it remained a delicate bit of business. To make good on his promise, Ambassador Rooney would need the tacit approval of Louis Susman, ambassador to Britain, and his and my father's boss, Secretary of State Hillary Clinton. But he decided on the spot that Marshall was onto something—visiting all of Ireland's counties would make a statement about not only his tenure but also Washington's interest in the entire island of Ireland, the ancestral home of so many Americans.

He was determined to visit every corner of the island, because it meant that much to him, and he thought it would mean something to the Irish people. "I can see myself going around and doing things: talking to the people, having, you know, town halls," he told the senators. "I would try to go everywhere." He would listen to the people. It was one of his greatest strengths as a business leader, and it was a characteristic that marked him as a very different sort of diplomat.

The committee recommended Dan Rooney's approval and the full Senate confirmed his nomination. And so this descendant of Irish immigrants was off to Dublin to represent the people and government of the United States.

Dan and my mother, Patricia, settled into a grand home in Dublin's magnificent Phoenix Park that was once the residence of the chief secretary of Ireland, the top British civil servant on the island. The home, called the Deerfield Residence, is adjacent to an even grander building that once upon a time was called the Viceregal Lodge and housed the lord lieutenant of Ireland, who represented the British monarch. It is now the home of Ireland's president and is called Áras an Uachtaráin. Dan would soon develop a wonderful working relationship with his neighbors, President Mary McAleese and her husband, Martin McAleese.

The Ireland that greeted Ambassador Rooney in 2009 was a very different place than it was when the American Ireland Fund was formed in the 1970s to encourage investment on both sides of the Irish border. The North was at peace, although that peace remained fragile. The Irish Republic had witnessed significant economic growth, a far cry from the stagnant malaise of 30 years earlier. It was no longer poor by Western standards and technologically backward, thanks in part to investment from the United States and the European Union.

But a year before Ambassador Rooney's arrival in Ireland, the country plunged into a deep recession. One of the country's most prominent financial institutions, Anglo-Irish Bank, failed spectacularly. Unemployment began to spike up again to double digits, the government was forced to cut back spending, and once again young Irish people were beginning to leave. The Celtic Tiger was dead of overindulgence by 2009.

Jake Sullivan, who served as deputy chief of staff to Hillary Clinton while she was secretary of state, recalled that Dan was determined to do what he could to lift the spirits of the Irish people. They felt as though their institutions had let them down—banks had loaned money irresponsibly, governments had spent recklessly and even the traditional rock of Irish culture and tradition, the Catholic Church, had lost its moral authority after a series of sexual abuse scandals.

"He arrived in Dublin at a moment when Ireland was flat on its back," Sullivan said. "The financial crisis crushed Ireland in every way—economically, of course, but it also crushed them psychologically. And so he saw one of his jobs to be someone who could help with the spirit of the people of Ireland—to help point the way to a more positive future, but also to think about what he could do from the point of view of foreign investment in projects that could help jump-start economic growth and dynamism."

For Dan, it was all about identifying realistic goals and mobilizing the support needed to achieve them. He was not about to let red tape or ancient protocol get in the way of his stated goal of listening to all sides of Ireland's disputes, of doing his best to put the United States on the right side of history in Ireland, and of ensuring that American interests and Irish interests were in alignment. If that meant crossing borders, symbolic and real, so be it.

"I knew a lot of ambassadors from a lot of countries, both career foreign service officers and political appointees, and there was nobody who had an instinctive skill for public diplomacy and the importance of the ambassador not just being a link to the government, but to the people of the country he or she was serving in than Dan Rooney," Sullivan added. "The fact that he went to all 32 counties was not just some box-checking exercise. It was a statement of respect and deep feeling for all of the people of Ireland."

Not long into his tenure as ambassador, he put up a map of Ireland on a wall in his study in the ambassador's residence. Every time he visited a new county, a green pin was planted on the appropriate spot on the map. Soon there were red pins as well—they represented the places where he held town hall meetings.

There were other kinds of boundaries that my father sought to cross—the boundaries that divided neighbors in Northern Ireland. He was determined to explore those boundaries even if he couldn't break them down entirely.

It started with a series of meetings, what Ambassador Rooney described as fireside chats, in the ambassador's residence with business leaders, shop owners, clergy, laborers, and community activists from the North, Protestant and Catholic alike. He made a point of ensuring that these meetings included people from the North who knew what it was like to live in poverty, to feel cast aside by the new economy of the 21st century. "The ambassador deliberately and specifically took the time to talk to these representatives [of the community], bring them together, and point out that the U.S. would continue to be there for them," said Sullivan.

It would be hard to overstate the importance of these meetings in the ongoing process of building trust, easing tensions and, to be sure, breaking down boundaries. Members of Northern Ireland's Unionist and Loyalist communities had long regarded any Irish-American as instinctively supportive of a united Ireland, which the Unionists and Loyalists opposed, and hostile to anything they would have to say. But they soon discovered that in Dan Rooney, they had somebody who was willing not simply to show up and nod, but to listen to their stories and their grievances. And that open-mindedness, that ability to once again put aside the accepted way of doing things in pursuit of doing the right thing, led the Protestant community to rethink its impressions not only of the United States, but of the Irish Republic as well.

The visits to the ambassador's residence had another benefit, thanks to geography. Martin McAleese, who was born in Northern Ireland, was heavily involved in these meetings, and after they were over, he invited the visitors from the North to stop by the president's residence nearby, to meet with his wife, Mary McAleese. Those meetings with the Irish president would not have taken place in isolation, Martin McAleese said. The Unionist and Loyalist leaders represented people who had been raised to think of the Irish Republic as something other than a friendly neighbor. The community's leaders "could not justify to their constituents that they were visiting the president of Ireland," Martin McAleese said. "It was just too large of a challenge. Because of Dan, however, what they could do was visit the U.S. ambassador as their main purpose. They had business with him, and then, 'by the way,' they can get the president [of Ireland] as a simple gesture of courtesy. These visits were enormously helpful for Irish relations with the Unionists."

Even though the peace process had taken hold in the North and had turned onetime enemies into partners, the idea of sending former Loyalist gunmen to the United States was immensely controversial on both sides of the Atlantic. By this point, John Hume and his Social Democratic and Labour Party had faded as a political force in the North and as a presence in the United States. Gerry Adams and his Sinn Fein party dominated the narrative in the United States, telling a story Irish-Americans wanted to hear. There was little evidence that Irish America wanted to hear about the grievances of other groups in Northern Ireland.

But McAleese and Rooney believed it was essential to bring all parties into the discussion of Northern Ireland's future. The Loyalists felt forgotten—obviously the province's Catholics did not speak for them, but neither did the Unionists, who tended to be more affluent, better-educated and immune from the factory closings that had decimated blue-collar Northern Ireland. "In close cooperation with McAleese, the ambassador reached out to people who had been paramilitary, who had been involved in the Troubles, but questioning, perhaps, the logic of having given up the gun," said John Hennessey-Niland, who was the charge d'affaires (the number two official at an embassy) in Dublin for my father.

Sullivan, who worked on this initiative in his role at the State Department, said Ambassador Rooney wanted to make sure that Loyalists had a chance to meet with Americans on American soil. That, Sullivan said, would allow them to "feel respect, that they have a voice, that they have a constituency in the United States that's supporting them in their work."

This was something close to heresy among many in the Irish-American community. But Rooney understood, as others did as well, that the old ways and the old narratives had to be changed in order for the Irish people to move forward. "Dan was really, really committed to this, and raised this with senior levels, and said, 'You know, I want to make sure we get this done,' " Sullivan recalled. "For him, it was fundamentally about the personal dimension of peace. That you show people dignity. And not just on one side, but on both sides." That perspective was like a breath of fresh air in international relations.

Dan Rooney and Martin McAleese had to get agreement from their bosses— Hillary Clinton, of course, was my father's, and Martin's was his wife, the president of Ireland. At a late-night meeting at the ambassador's residence in Dublin, Secretary Clinton, President McAleese, Martin and Dan designed their strategy.

One of the Loyalists who had attended Ambassador Rooney's fireside chats in the residence, Jackie McDonald, was the leader of a Protestant / Loyalist paramilitary group called the Ulster Defense Association. Working in cooperation with Martin McAleese, Dan decided that McDonald and three other UDA members should be allowed to go to America to tell their stories.

They flew over in early October 2011, met with a number of U.S. officials and toured economic development projects underway in Washington and in Newark, N.J. They told their American hosts of their own community's economic difficulties—blue-collar workers in Northern Ireland, Protestant and Catholic alike—were suffering just as much as those in the old industrialized areas of the United States. "They had never heard anything from the Loyalist working-class perspective before," McDonald later said. There were many parallels, he said, between the unemployed and underemployed American workers and the out-of-work Loyalists of Northern Ireland.

Ambassador Rooney recognized the economic plight the Loyalists faced because he knew of the hardships faced by his fellow Americans in western Pennsylvania and other parts of the old industrial heartland of America. The two groups felt alienated, culturally and economically, and were frustrated that nobody seemed to be listening to them. But Dan heard them.

"We were welcome in America, thanks to Dan Rooney," McDonald said. "He gave us the opportunities that no one ever gave us before."

Similar to my father's beliefs related to providing opportunities to minorities in sports, he also felt that if people were given opportunities in Ireland, peace was possible. Now, as ambassador, he was creating those opportunities and was witnessing the results firsthand.

"The ambassador was willing to take risks," said Hennessey-Niland. "He would bring people together who would not normally talk to each other. But because it was Ambassador Rooney, because it was in the privacy of the ambassador's residence in Phoenix Park, and because of the respect people have on both sides of the ocean for the Rooney family, people came together and talked."

Hennessey-Niland summed up Ambassador Rooney's style as ambassador: "Be ready for criticism but do the right thing. Do the bold thing, both publicly and privately, to find common ground. He was determined to make a mark, and not for himself, but for the greater good."

For anyone who had followed Rooney's career as an NFL owner and business-man, that description would have sounded familiar.

There was quiet diplomacy, the kind that led to the Loyalist visit to the U.S., and then there was the public side of diplomacy, in which Dan (like any U.S. ambassador in any country) served as the face of America—and the representa-tive of America's interests—in a foreign land. Of course, Ireland was not exactly "foreign" for Dan Rooney. But he understood that as much as he cherished his Irish heritage and the people of the island, he was an American whose job it was to project his country's image and interests.

The American Embassy in Dublin had for years celebrated the Fourth of July with great fanfare. There's always a party at the residence in Phoenix Park, to which top Irish officials as well as Americans in Ireland are invited. My father expanded the celebration, adding something very all-American to the day's activities: Football, of course.

Actually, it was flag football, with men and women who worked at the U.S. Embassy—including several U.S. Marines—against a coed group of Irish athletes, most of whom played rugby or Gaelic football. The expansive green grounds surrounding the ambassador's residence made for a perfect setting. Staff from the embassy and from Dublin's premier outdoor arena, Croke Park, laid out the playing field. Much like an NFL stadium, this field would have the marking of the home team at midfield. In this case it was the seal of the United States prominently displayed at the 50-yard line, something that would make any American football fan proud. They also put up goal posts, and constructed bleachers and a press box. A jumbotron completed the effect of turning a corner of Dublin's huge Phoenix Park into a reasonable facsimile of the Super Bowl. Before the main event, there was a family game for kids.

Ambassador Rooney ensured that all of these events were subsidized through corporate sponsorship. No taxpayer dollars were used.

"It was so American," said Katie Keogh, a senior staffer at the U.S. Embassy in Dublin, "It wasn't even just the single day. We had the coaches in meetings six or seven weeks out. It was six, seven weeks of training, two or three days a week, meetings with the ambassador. It was all extremely serious, but it was also just so much fun."

At one level, the Fourth of July celebration was literally fun and games, but at a more profound level, it was about bringing together people from two nations and many backgrounds on, literally, a common ground. And it served as a point of contact between the business leaders who underwrote the activities and the embassy, to the benefit of both Ireland and the United States.

"I would say over the three years I worked with the ambassador, we probably quadrupled the number of contacts we had in our database," said Keogh. The touch football game became a highlight of the embassy's social calendar, something beyond the customary rituals of public diplomacy.

Sometimes my father was willing to share his insights at unusual hours. One night—actually, it was 3 o'clock in the morning—the phone rang in the ambassador's residence. It was Bono—yes, the lead singer of U2—looking to speak with Ambassador Rooney. "I don't even remember what my grievance was," Bono told me following U2's first concert at Heinz Field after the passing of my father in 2017. I'm not going to pretend he and Bono were best friends, but they actually had connected several times over the previous 30 years and his condolences and affection couldn't have been more heartfelt. He continued with his story, saying that he roused Dan from his sleep. "He gets on the phone in the middle of the night, listened to me complain for a bit, then in his disarming way we settle into a conversation until dawn," Bono recalled. "I will always remember his kindness and unwavering commitment to peace in my homeland."

Most people probably don't think of Ireland as particularly diverse—for hundreds of years, Ireland was known for producing, rather than attracting, immigrants. But the Ireland of the 21st century is very different from the Ireland of past centuries, even of the Ireland of the 1990s. The Celtic Tiger's roaring economy came to a crashing halt just before Rooney got there, but while it was roaring, it not only kept the Irish at home but, for the first time, immigrants arrived in significant numbers looking for a better life.

Ambassador Rooney recognized the changes in Ireland because they reflected the changes he had witnessed in the United States since the 1970s. He knew the challenges that accompany changes in demographics and culture, and he sought to use his position as the representative of one of the world's most diverse democracies to foster toleration in Ireland.

Muslims were and remain a tiny minority in Ireland, but their presence in the nation's daily life has increased significantly in the 21st century. There were only about 4,000 Muslims in the country in 1991. Within 20 years, the number rose to nearly 50,000, about half of whom lived in or near Dublin. They faced all of the problems that minority populations around the world face. Dan sought to use his office and influence to help ease any tensions or misunderstandings between Ireland's overwhelmingly Catholic population and its small but visible minority.

He met often with leaders of mosques, and he hosted an interfaith lunch that brought together Catholic, Protestant, Jewish and Muslim clergy—in the latter case, from both the Sunni and Shi'a traditions—to help find common ground and to get a conversation going. That particular outreach, said Keogh, was part of Ambassador Rooney's broader vision of the position he held and the influence he could bring to the table in the pursuit of civility and mutual respect.

"He could have taken a different approach with all this and not worked as hard and not hosted as many events," she said. "But he did them, and with his tireless energy, he transformed the position."

Events like the interfaith lunches crossed any number of borders—they helped to foster understanding among religious groups, they helped create a dialogue among Irish people, and they added to my father's most important mission: to advance the interests and reputation of the United States through diplomacy, civil discourse and personal engagement.

He made sure that the man who appointed him—President Obama—was kept informed of all of this activity, but he did so in his own unique way.

He sent the president postcards.

He respected the president's time and priorities, and he was pretty old-fashioned anyway. So rather than bother the president with phone calls or even emails (which would have presented their own challenges), he would jot down a few thoughts on the front of a postcard and send them to the White House via the president's aide, Reggie Love. On the back of the postcards, of course, were lovely pictures of Ireland.

When one of those postcards landed on Love's desk, he walked it into the Oval Office and put it on the president's desk. "How old school is that?" said Hennessey-Niland. "But it beat all the emails and it beat all the phone calls, because it was personal from the ambassador to the president."

On May 23, 2011, my father greeted the president and First Lady Michelle Obama as they stepped off Air Force One at Dublin Airport for a whirlwind

12-hour visit that was one of the highlights of my father's tenure as ambassador. (Another highlight took place a week earlier, when Queen Elizabeth II became the first monarch to visit Ireland since 1911, and both of my parents met her.)

When President Obama spoke to Ireland, the Irish greeted him as if he were one of their own. Which, as he reminded the crowd, he was. "I'm Barack Obama," he said. "From the Moneygall Obamas." It was true—his great-great-great-grandfather, Falmouth Kearney, was born in the village of Moneygall in County Offaly, and left for America as a young man in 1850, about the same time James Rooney left Newry to begin our family's journey to America.

Moneygall in 2011 was a town of about 300 people with a couple of stores, a couple of churches and a couple of pubs. But thousands lined the streets that day, even though it was a wet and windy Irish day, when the president of the United States came to town to discover his Irish roots on his mother's side. The president and the first lady shook hundreds of hands on the other side of barricades set up along the town's main street. "He met everybody in town," Dan recalled in an interview.

Just as memorable, in a different way, were Ambassador Rooney's trips to Shannon airport in the west of Ireland. The airport was and is an important economic engine in a rural part of the country. But it also was important for U.S. strategic interests, for it served as a critical refueling stop for military planes making their way to and from the war zones in Iraq and Afghanistan. This would be the final stop in the Western Hemisphere for soldiers on their way to war and the first stop back for those returning from the conflict. Dan regularly visited the airport to connect with troops and support staff, making sure they knew how much he, and the nation, appreciated their service and sacrifice.

His insistence on showing appreciation for everyone involved in an enterprise—whether it was running a football franchise or representing the United States in a foreign country—reflected his upbringing and the values he brought to the fields of business, sports and diplomacy. People noticed, and they in turn appreciated what he did for them.

Katie Keogh recalled: "He looked after us as people and as if we were part of his family. I think that's what inspired everybody to do more for him."

After President Obama was re-elected to a second term in 2012, my father decided it was time to return home. He resigned in December of that year, content that he had achieved the goals he had in mind when he arrived. He helped move along the peace process, he connected American businesses to opportunities in Ireland, and he moved the relationship between Ireland and the United States beyond Dublin and into the villages and homes of the Irish people themselves. Through those visits, personal appearances and quiet words of encouragement, he instilled a sense of hope to an island scarred by violence and economic despair. The echo of Obama's 2008 campaign slogan may have been coincidental, but it certainly was appropriate.

"People who would have never met an ambassador met Dan Rooney," recalled Seamus Mallon. "He was very proud of visiting all 32 counties. He knew that there were many ordinary, decent people whose lives were not centered on the cities." They, too, had a voice, and Ambassador Daniel Rooney made sure they were heard.

The Ireland he left in December 2012 was well on its way to economic recovery after the disaster that followed the collapse of the Celtic Tiger. Projects he had helped to fund and nurture had matured, the peace process continued to hold and, more than anything else, there was a sense of hope on both sides of the Irish border.

"If there was one word I associated with Dan, it would be 'hope,' " Mallon said.

Hope was in short supply in Ireland when the Rooneys left Newry in the 19th century. When the Rooneys left Dublin almost two centuries later, hope no longer seemed so elusive. Decades of hard work and quiet determination helped make it so.

Dan Rooney and Tayyibah Taylor | U.S. State Department

Ambassador Rooney, Patricia Rooney, President Obama, President McAleese, Martin McAleese, Michelle Obama | U.S. State Department

Kip Condron, Peter Robinson, Loretta Brennan Glucksman, Martin McGuinness, Dan Rooney
Aengus McMahon/The Ireland Funds

Senator George Mitchell, Dan Rooney, Kieran McLoughlin
Michael Nagle/The Ireland Funds

Patricia Rooney, Sir Tony O'Reilly, Dan Rooney | Aengus McMahon/The Ireland Funds

President Obama and Ambassador Rooney in the Oval Office "with the football" | Pete Souza

Dan Rooney and Capricia Marshall | Charles Dharapak/Associated Press

Dan Rooney and Patricia Rooney visiting U.S. troops in Ireland | U.S. State Department

Dan Rooney and Patricia Rooney | Rooney Family

CONCLUSION

The island of Ireland has been transformed since the terrible days of the 1970s, thanks in part to the intervention, hard work and vision of Irish America. The American Ireland Fund has raised more than $600 million since its inception, under the leadership of Tony O'Reilly, my father and so many others. It now has chapters in a dozen countries. Hundreds of projects have been funded with money raised at events around the globe.

The Republic of Ireland is a modern European country with a 21st century economy. It was brought to its knees with the worldwide economic collapse of 2008, but today it continues to attract companies seeking a well-educated English-speaking workforce. U.S.-based multinational companies, from Bank of America to Merrill Lynch to Google to Intel, have developed a significant presence in Ireland since the 1970s. Unemployment reached an astonishing 20 percent in the 1980s; in early 2019, the jobless rate was about 5 percent.

And, of course, peace has taken hold in Northern Ireland. Power-sharing and reconciliation remain imperfect, but in the second decade of the 21st century, an entire generation of Catholics and Protestants has known nothing but peace. Unemployment in the North has gone down from about 17 percent in the 1980s to about 6 percent in 2019. Political leaders who were ready to kill each other in the late 20th century worked together to strengthen the peace process in the new century.

It was difficult for anyone to see such an outcome in the late 1970s. But by taking the long view, by appealing to others to compromise and to do the right thing by the people they represent, my father helped make the land of his ancestors a better, more prosperous and peaceful place.

MINORITY HIRES
BEFORE
&
AFTER
THE ROONEY RULE

THE ROONEY RULE
THE ROONEY RULE
THE ROONEY RULE
THE ROONEY RULE
THE ROONEY RULE
THE ROONEY RULE
THE ROONEY RULE
THE ROONEY RULE

Tom Flores

Tony Dungy

Art Shell

Dennis Green

Ray Rhodes

Herm Edwards

Fritz Pollard

STORY IV | VOCATION

Harris Mike Tomlin Raheem Morris Mike Singletary Hue Jackson Steve Wilks

Marvin Lewis Ozzie Newsome Romeo Crennel Doug Whaley Todd Bowles Rick Smith

Jerry Reese Jim Caldwell Leslie Frazier Rod Graves Herm Edwards Brian Flores

Ray Farmer Martin Mayhew Ron Rivera Art Shell Doug Williams Sashi Brown

e Smith Dennis Green Reggie McKenzie Anthony Lynn Vance Joseph Chris Grier

HEAD COACHES & GENERAL MANAGERS SINCE 2003

HIS LIFE'S WORK—
THE ROONEY RULE

STORY IV | VOCATION:
HIS LIFE'S WORK—THE ROONEY RULE

A young man who would go on to have an extraordinary influence over my father's thinking arrived in Pittsburgh in the early 1960s. The young man never put on a pair of shoulder pads or a helmet, and had no idea what it was like to throw a block or make an open-field tackle. But he shared something very important with the NFL: His busiest day of the week was Sunday.

Father Mark Glasgow was ordained a Roman Catholic priest in 1962 and was assigned to my parents' parish church. Father Glasgow was part of a generation of young priests eager to apply the lessons they learned in the seminary to the problems and injustices of modern life. His homilies were filled with references to the struggle for civil rights as it unfolded through the early 1960s, led by Dr. Martin Luther King Jr. Father Glasgow made it clear that the messages contained in the Gospels he proclaimed at Mass were more than simply old stories handed down through the generations. They were a call to action, he said.

My father, now in his early 30s, was already involved in the Urban League and the NAACP chapters in Pittsburgh. But Father Glasgow's homilies and private conversations persuaded him that he could be doing more. "Father Glasgow's preaching—it hit him between the eyes," my mother recalled.

Father Glasgow was a member of the city's Catholic Interracial Council, and in 1965, after civil rights workers and advocates were beaten and, in several cases, murdered, he and a couple of other priests went to Selma, Alabama. Father Glasgow invited him to join. In a decision that my father would regularly refer to as the biggest mistake of his life, he did not go.

With true guilt (not the vacuous kind that most Catholics carry), he realized he was wrong. It was his fight, and he wasn't there. Father Glasgow's homilies about his own activism in Selma undoubtedly contributed to my father's thinking, and many years later, he still often spoke about the missed opportunity to travel to Selma in 1965.

There certainly was a silver lining: this spiritual dimension that propelled his sense of regret and drove him to become more active in helping to right wrongs for the rest of his life. It led to a change in the way the Steelers scouted and built their rosters. It informed his work in Ireland and, most important, it influenced the thinking behind what would become known as the Rooney Rule, which requires NFL teams to interview minority candidates for head coaching and senior football operations jobs.

My father spent his professional life as a sports executive and public figure working to expand opportunities for people who were overlooked. When the lack of diversity among NFL coaches became a crisis, the effort to address the issue became the last great test of his ability to balance idealism and pragmatism.

He did not see broadening a candidate pool for coaches as necessitating a lowering of standards. Rather, he wanted the NFL to consider more minority coaches because it was the right thing to do, and because he believed they might do a better job than those who were being hired. He was troubled by what he perceived as the laziness of some owners who would not consider a broader pool of candidates. It was, he believed, an outgrowth of the financial success so many owners had enjoyed—they no longer saw the need to go the extra mile.

My father also understood that head coach hirings were private business decisions made by fiercely independent executives, because he was one of them.

A change in approach this significant is difficult in the NFL, as it is in any organization. And there would be some resistance.

He had been wrestling with how to make changes and how to convince others to join him in those changes throughout his life. Jeff Pash, the NFL lawyer, often recalls one of the aphorisms my father referred to during years of labor battles— that sometimes things have to get worse before they get better. And my mom still speaks of my dad's ability to visualize projects and have the determination to get them done. That perseverance made an impression on Joe Greene, just as my dad's knack for building consensus did on Katie Keogh at the embassy in Dublin.

My father would bring all of those qualities—the credibility he had built in the NFL, the ability to forge common ground, and his willingness to immerse himself in the nitty-gritty of the process and continue to be a champion for what he believed in—to improve opportunities for minority coaches in the NFL. The Rooney Rule would be the culmination of his life's work and his professional approach.

TEN

PAVING THE WAY

Cyrus Mehri followed his usual habit on a mid-January morning in 2002, reading The Washington Post's sports section first. Tony Dungy had been fired the day before as head coach of the Tampa Bay Buccaneers, after the Bucs lost to the Philadelphia Eagles in a wild card playoff game. The firing felt awfully familiar to Mehri, who was still upset that Dennis Green had been let go by the Minnesota Vikings little more than a week earlier, three weeks before the final game of the regular season.

Mehri is a Washington, D.C., attorney, a protégé of Ralph Nader and a titan in the fight against workplace discrimination. He is also a rabid football fan.

So Mehri knew well the history of Green and Dungy. Green, just the second African-American head coach hired by an NFL team, was fired as the Vikings were about to miss the playoffs for only the second time in his 10 seasons.

Dungy, the former Steelers player and defensive coordinator and one of my father's favorites, had taken over one of the league's doormats and made them a perennial contender. With a formidable defense, the Bucs went to the playoffs in four of Dungy's six seasons—including one appearance in the NFC Championship Game—and they were in the playoffs in his last three straight seasons.

Dungy's firing was particularly stark given the long history of futility that preceded him. Before Dungy was hired, five different coaches combined to lead 13 consecutive losing seasons.

Dungy's only losing season as the Bucs' coach—indeed, the only losing season in his entire 13-year head coaching career, which landed him in the Pro Football Hall of Fame—was his very first. Dan thought that there were a lot of coaches hired who were simply not on Dungy's level, either as a coach or as a person. He thought so highly of Dungy that he pushed Tagliabue to hire Dungy for a job in the league office.

That Dungy and Green led consistent playoff contenders but lacked the kind of job security that many of their less accomplished—but white—peers enjoyed was not lost on Mehri. Some in the NFL hierarchy were aware there was a problem, too, even before Dungy and Green caught Mehri's attention. The NFL was the last of the big three U.S. sports leagues to promote an African-American to its highest coaching job in modern times. Art Shell, the Hall of Fame offensive lineman, was named the head coach of the Los Angeles Raiders in October 1989, 23 years after Bill Russell became the first black NBA coach and 15 years after Frank Robinson became Major League Baseball's first black manager.

NFL leaders had already put in place a collection of initiatives to help boost the careers of minority candidates. Dan had been a proponent of those efforts within ownership circles.

A visitation program was established in 1979 to provide NFL-funded opportunities for coaches from HBCUs to shadow NFL coaches during training camps. In 1987, the late Hall of Fame Coach Bill Walsh established a minority coaching fellowship to provide training camp positions to minority coaches every year. Mike Tomlin, Lovie Smith, Herm Edwards and Marvin Lewis—all of whom became NFL head coaches—are among the nearly 2,000 coaches who have participated in the fellowship program. And in January 1998, Tagliabue penned an op-ed in The New York Times, in which he lamented the lack of minority hires.

"All of us in football—professional and college—must do better in identifying top coaching talent from a diverse, growing pool, including African-Americans and those from other minority groups," Tagliabue wrote. "It is both the right thing and the smart thing to do."

Later that year, after there had been just one minority candidate during that year's hiring cycle, Tagliabue brought in an international executive search firm, Russell Reynolds Associates, led by former Cowboys executive Joe Bailey. They found that many coaching hires are made based on recommendations from successful and respected people in the league. But with few minority coaches in those influential circles of power, the NFL hiring process looked very much like an old boys' club. The coaching trees that give owners the comfort of an endorsement from someone they trust were notably monochromatic.

Russell Reynolds helped the NFL develop a videotape interview program that allowed assistant coaches—black and white—to be interviewed on tape by a professional search firm. The team owner or club president could then get a better idea of who was available before in-person interviews began, enhancing familiarity with a wider range of candidates.

All of those ideas were well-intentioned and made some inroads. But there was no coherent plan under one umbrella and none of the programs required the participation of teams. And, ironically, because Rooney was working hard to improve minority opportunities, because he was so close to Dungy, Gene Upshaw and others who were on the forefront of this issue, he may have missed how much bigger the problem had become by the time Dungy and Green were fired.

After reading about Dungy, Mehri thought it was time to pressure the NFL to make its hiring practices more inclusive, the same way he had pursued corporate behemoths like Texaco and Coca-Cola with lawsuits that resulted in nine-figure settlements and diversity task forces to monitor hiring practices. He wanted statistical evidence to prove to NFL owners that racial discrimination was hindering black coaches' careers and—to really appeal to owners' competitive streak—that teams were also paying the price with poorer results because of their reluctance to hire them.

Mehri commissioned a study by University of Pennsylvania sociology professor Janice Madden, a specialist in the study of discrimination in the labor market, to compare the performance of the NFL's five black head coaches to the performance of the 86 white head coaches who had coached between 1986 and 2001.

The results would not be pretty, surprising even my father. But the issue Mehri raised was the catalyst—something he recognized almost immediately—for what would become the final stamp Dan would help put on the NFL. His belief in equal opportunity and inclusion had been threaded throughout his life, from the earliest days in his neighborhood to his hiring practices with the Steelers and his efforts in Ireland. It had not been a smooth arc. Just as in the NFL, the slow pace of change among some other owners was an enduring source of frustration for my father.

Before Shell, the most recent black man to be an NFL coach was Fritz Pollard, for whom the alliance that promotes diversity in NFL coaching and executive ranks was named. Pollard was a player-coach during the early 1920s, in the NFL's infancy. As the league blossomed and then boomed around them for more than six decades, black coaches were left behind. It was an appalling omission in the otherwise staggering success of the league.

At the press conference announcing his promotion, Shell recognized that Raiders owner Al Davis had made him a pioneer.

"It is an historic event. I understand the significance of it," Shell said that day at a news conference. "I'm proud of it, but I'm also a Raider. I don't believe the color of my skin entered into this decision. I was chosen because Al Davis felt I was the right person at the right time."

Which, of course, was exactly what Mehri was hoping his groundbreaking study would encourage more owners to do.

By September 2002, when Mehri's report was ready, there were just two active black head coaches—Edwards, in his second year at the Jets, and Dungy, who had been hired by the Indianapolis Colts soon after the Bucs fired him. On September 30, just hours before the Broncos were to play the Ravens on Monday Night Football, Mehri and famed attorney Johnnie Cochran Jr. announced the findings at a press conference in Baltimore.

The report, titled "Black Coaches in the National Football League: Superior Performance, Inferior Opportunities," was damning. And it landed like a thunderbolt.

Madden had found that black head coaches won a higher percentage of games but were less likely to be hired and were more quickly fired than their white counterparts. Black coaches averaged 9.1 victories per season while white coaches averaged eight wins. During the 15-year span studied, that one extra win made a world of difference—60 percent of teams that won nine games in a season advanced to the playoffs while only 10 percent of teams that won eight games went to the playoffs. Black coaches also averaged 2.7 more wins in their first season with their teams than did white coaches. And black coaches outperformed white coaches in their last seasons before being fired, averaging 1.3 more victories in their final season than white coaches.

Plus, black coaches were grossly underrepresented. At the time of the report, about 70 percent of players in the league were black. Just six percent of head coaches were black. And only 28 percent of coordinators—a frequent feeder pool for head coaches—were black.

For years, Dan had felt he and others were working hard to improve opportunities in the NFL and he thought that his and Tagliabue's personal interest in diversity made them leaders. The results of Madden's study hit him to his core. He was upset and even a little disillusioned about how little progress the NFL had made.

The report used Dungy's career arc to illustrate the problem. It noted that Dungy was overlooked for head coaching opportunities in the first 15 years of his coaching career despite successful stints on the defensive staff for the Steelers, Chiefs and Vikings. Then, when he was finally hired by the Bucs, he was fired after six successful seasons.

Dungy entered the league as a Steelers rookie in 1977 and remained close to my father from then on. Dungy recalls there were perhaps 10 African-American coaches throughout the league—and none of them head coaches. There were simply not many role models then for young African-American coaches. Bill Nunn used to tell Dungy not to be in a rush to leave the Steelers for other opportunities, because the Steelers were one of the few teams then with a clear commitment to having a diverse staff. When Dungy became a Steelers defensive assistant coach in 1981, at 25 the youngest assistant in league history at that time, he was only number 14 or 15 of African-American coaches. It was agonizingly incremental improvement.

Around that time, George Young, the New York Giants general manager and a friend of Dungy's, advised Dungy to shave his beard if he wanted to get jobs in the conservative NFL, because, with that beard, Dungy looked more like a player than the prototypical coach in a buttoned-down league.

Dungy asked Dan about it and got different advice. " 'Here, we like people to be who they are,' " Dungy remembers my father telling him. " 'Don't ever feel like you have to change your appearance.' "

When Dungy became the Steelers' defensive coordinator in 1984 at age 29, he was the youngest and first African-American defensive coordinator in NFL history. By then, Dungy had started to wonder who would be—or if there would be—the first black head coach in the NFL. When Chuck Noll made changes to his staff after the Steelers finished 5-11 in 1988—some changes at the behest of Rooney—Dungy left to be the defensive backs coach for the Chiefs. He was only 34 and Shell was still months away from being named the Raiders' head coach.

When Shell did get the job in the middle of the 1989 season, Dungy thought surely that the barrier finally falling would open the door to numerous African-American coaches who had been in the league a long time.

It would be another three years before Green became the second black head coach, when he went to Minnesota in 1992. And he hired Dungy to be his defensive coordinator. That same year, the Steelers were looking for a new head coach after Chuck Noll's retirement. Joe Greene was a candidate and he was frustrated he did not get the job. The Steelers won a Super Bowl with the man who did get the job, Bill Cowher. Dungy understood both Greene's importance to the franchise and Cowher's skills from working with him in Kansas City, so he wasn't bothered that he wasn't interviewed.

Wherever he went, Dungy stayed in constant touch with Nunn back in Pittsburgh. Nunn knew well Dungy's concerns about the landscape for minority coaches. Nunn's advice to Dungy was simple: Don't get discouraged by the process. Just make sure you are doing everything you can to get yourself ready. Green, meanwhile, was also helping Dungy get ready, bringing him into meetings, giving him access to information and decisions head coaches had to make, offering insight to which other assistants were not always privy.

After the 1993 season, though, Dungy had his first real doubts about the hiring process. The Vikings defense he coordinated was the top-ranked defense in the league that season. And there were five head coaching openings.

Dungy remembers thinking at that time with a hint of sarcasm, "Gosh, it doesn't seem like owners would cut their nose off to spite their face. You would think they would want what's best."

Dungy did not get even one interview. Or even a phone call. Or any sign that any team was even thinking about him.

"It wasn't even close to happening," Dungy remembers. "That was the one time I got a little discouraged."

The next year, Dungy did get an interview, with the Philadelphia Eagles. The Eagles ended up hiring Ray Rhodes, but Dungy felt better about the process—the Eagles had run an inclusive search and had picked the man, a black man it so happened, who they believed was best for the job. Dungy thought he was back on track, but he still looked at the timeline. Shell had been hired in 1989, Green in 1992, Rhodes in 1995.

"You think, this is a slow pace," Dungy said.

Finally, in 1996, then-Buccaneers general manager Rich McKay asked to interview Dungy. McKay had spent his entire life around the NFL as the youngest son of the Bucs' first coach, John McKay.

"It was strictly Rich McKay growing up in a football household and playing against us twice a year, knowing my players and what they said about me," Dungy said. "He wondered, why aren't we looking at this guy? When he interviewed me, one of the questions he asked was, you've had all these interviews, why do you think you did not get the job?

"I said, 'I haven't had many interviews, I have had four.' He said, that can't be, it has to be 20 or 30.

" 'No, I've had four.' "

Once he got the job, Dungy made a conscious decision to hire people, particularly young African-Americans, who were not already well-established in the NFL coaching pipeline. Among those who worked for Dungy in Tampa were Lovie Smith, Herm Edwards and Mike Tomlin, all of whom became head coaches, creating one of the league's most historically significant coaching trees.

Dan was a mentor throughout Dungy's career. The Steelers had provided the beginning of Dungy's playing and coaching careers, and Dan had championed Dungy for a job at the league office to give him greater insight into and exposure throughout the NFL. And the two had an ongoing conversation that stretched for years about the effort that eventually became the Rooney Rule.

Their bond helped Dungy persevere until he finally became a head coach. Still, Dungy had been a victim of the systemic problem Madden's study had so starkly revealed: There was a gridiron glass ceiling.

Madden's conclusion summed up what Dungy and so many others had experienced: "No matter how we look at success, black coaches are performing better. These data are consistent with blacks having to be better coaches than the whites in order to get a job as head coach in the NFL."

Sure enough, Cochran, the attorney whose fame brought even greater attention to Madden's report, knew what would focus everybody's attention on this issue.

" 'If you don't negotiate, we'll litigate,' " Mehri recalls Cochran saying at the press conference to announce Madden's findings. "All of a sudden, we were everywhere."

ELEVEN

CREDIBILITY

NO MATTER THEIR KNOWLEDGE OF FOOTBALL, owners of NFL teams have been nearly uniformly successful in business. And they learned the importance of having credibility with partners when confronting major challenges in their business. During decades of working with other team owners to navigate some of the most complex issues the NFL faced, while also being a champion for equal opportunity, Dan Rooney had built up the credibility needed to lead the NFL's efforts after Professor Janice Madden's findings were revealed.

Within the NFL, the reaction to the Mehri and Cochran report was, predictably, complicated. Most owners' first concern was that the league not be sued. Pash, the NFL's general counsel whom Mehri calls one of the unsung heroes of the entire project, assured them that—like Mehri—he did not see a viable legal claim on the horizon.

Not surprisingly, owners were also reluctant to admit publicly that they had, consciously or subconsciously, discriminated against African-American coaches. They wanted to be perceived as being fair to their coaching staffs, just as they wanted to be seen as being fair to players.

But mostly, the owners' pushback came down to their worldview: They own the league and they didn't want anybody else telling them what they had to do, even if it was for a goal they agreed with. That, most definitely, included the demands laid out by the media-star Cochran, who, as Pash dryly noted, "was not the model guy for the average NFL owner."

Fortunately, there were a number of owners in the league who saw the report as the emotional push the NFL needed to finally address its diversity issues and to do so with some urgency. Dan Rooney was in that cohort. He recognized immediately that the risk of litigation was slim, but he thought the threat—and the presence of Cochran himself—could be a cudgel to force the NFL to stop and think about where it was on race and what more it could do beyond the informal network of seminars and meetings that had sprung up.

Years of collaboration between Dan and Paul Tagliabue had built a well of mutual trust and respect. They were aligned on the need for immediate and significant action in the wake of Madden's report and their efforts on diversity would follow a familiar pattern. Tagliabue frequently relied on Dan for wisdom and leadership among the owners. On diversity, Dan Rooney and Paul Tagliabue took the lead together on an issue that mattered deeply to both of them. They would not do it alone—the league office had a big hand in forging the rule—but Rooney would have to manage whatever resistance arose.

"It's almost as though he were the president of the United States and he would call on the majority leader in the Senate to make sure he could put the votes together for a specific set of legislation," Carmen Policy, the former president of the San Francisco 49ers and Cleveland Browns, said in describing the relationship between Tagliabue and my father. "Dan was the number one person the commissioner would call to go out and bring everybody together, and get the votes necessary."

Tagliabue's career had long demonstrated his own commitment to improving inclusion.

As a young lawyer at Covington & Burling, he took a pro bono case in 1969 representing 15 black gardeners who alleged they were discriminated against while working at the National Institutes of Health. The gardeners, many of whom were war veterans, had operated heavy equipment while in the military but were repeatedly turned down by the federal government for jobs involving heavy equipment, told they didn't have the skills and experience necessary.

The gardeners asserted that their white peers had fewer qualifications but were getting the jobs. Tagliabue won a settlement, when the court ordered the federal government to give back pay to its employees.

Later, he supported Tom Williamson, the firm's first African-American partner, on an internal campaign to drop South African Airways as the firm's client during apartheid. Williamson would later play a key role in the creation of the Rooney Rule.

And after their son Drew told them he is gay, Tagliabue and his wife, Chan, chose to speak out with Drew at the league office about having and supporting a gay child. After that meeting, several members of the NFL staff approached Tagliabue to tell him of their personal situations. "They said until that moment, they had never been willing to be open with their fellow employees, except in very limited ways, but now they felt like they were really welcome," Tagliabue recalled. "That their humanity and their individuality was being respected. And that they were, for the first time, really comfortable being an NFL employee."

Tagliabue had also diversified the executive staff at the league office. In his most public statement, he recommended pulling Super Bowl XXVII from Phoenix after Arizona refused to honor Martin Luther King Day.

Behind the scenes, Tagliabue had quietly taken steps to boost the profiles of minority coaches well before Mehri's report. Together with Rooney, he had conversations with Green, Dungy, Upshaw and John Wooten, a former NFL player and personnel executive who would later become the head of the Fritz Pollard Alliance. One hurdle faced by minority coaches, Tagliabue learned, was that they were not as well-known among owners and club presidents as the coordinators who were getting head coaching jobs. Owners—particularly those who are not closely involved with their teams or the league—often rely on buzz, and they, like fans, want to hire the "hot" candidates. Those hot candidates have name recognition.

Tagliabue spoke to the heads of the NFL's broadcast partners and urged them to have their announcers identify African-American assistant coaches by name during broadcasts. He didn't tell them to say anything good or bad, just to identify them. That was often how owners first heard of assistant coaches and came to view them as up-and-coming candidates.

Tagliabue also began the practice of having minority coordinators make presentations to the rules-making Competition Committee during league meetings. The members of the Competition Committee are among the most influential owners, team presidents and general managers in the entire league and exposure to them is critical for ambitious coaches.

Tagliabue and Dan were of like minds on Mehri's report. My father had never forgotten about his missed opportunity to go to Selma with Father Glasgow during the 1960s and he viewed Mehri's report as an opening to extend his belief in the benefits of inclusion beyond the Steelers and into the entire league.

Dan knew there would be resistance to a change, rooted in the independence of each team and owner. The league could not simply tell teams who to hire. But he and others believed the time had come for the NFL to stop hoping that goodwill would deliver the desired results on minority hiring.

That, it was painfully obvious, was not working. The league needed a coordinated and expanded commitment to diversity. It needed ways to make owners aware of minority candidates. It needed mechanisms to get those candidates prepared. And it needed a system to hold teams accountable if the decision-makers did not even consider minority candidates.

Dan Rooney was a focused and persistent businessman and that is what allowed him to be successful among his highly competitive peers. But his core belief in the goodness of people was deeply woven into his approach. That innocence sometimes blinded him. He believed that once it was made obvious to other owners that they would benefit from hiring minority candidates, they would do it. That they would prove him wrong on that point—over and over—aggravated and even disillusioned him.

His response to Madden's report, ultimately, was pragmatic. From his years of living through the fits and starts of everything from sharing revenue to free agency, he knew that owners would not allow themselves to be strong-armed into change. This could not be a top-down mandate. The owners had to have the prerogative to hire and fire the people they want for key jobs. He knew that if the owners accepted responsibility for addressing the issue, and developed the solution, it had a chance to be effective. From his own experience, he knew that until owners recognized the benefits of including minority candidates on their short lists, the problem would continue.

Just three weeks after the release of the report, Mehri met with league representatives, including Pash and Williamson, who headed Covington & Burling's employment and practices group (and who had once turned down a football scholarship to play for Bill Walsh at Stanford). Harold Henderson, the chairman of the league's management council, was there to represent the interests of the owners.

With the league's regularly scheduled owners' meeting just days away, Tagliabue and Rooney went to work. As with most negotiations, progress is made in private conversations, often far away from the cameras and spotlights. Tagliabue and Rooney hatched a plan that would be presented at the meeting. A new committee would be formed, the Committee on Workplace Diversity. Tagliabue told Dan that he would have to be the chairman of the committee if there was any hope for success. The Steelers' championships gave him credibility as a successful owner and having an inclusive hiring approach going all the way back to Nunn was an important bit of symbolism for the face of the league's diversity efforts. My father was not a braggart, but he understood his role and influence in the league. It is not clear which other senior owners could have effectively led this charge. He was also prepared to stay with his issue, because he knew from his own experience this would not be solved overnight.

As part of their plan, Dan sent Tagliabue a letter that would later be read during the meeting, the contents of which had already been arranged between the league office and Rooney.

"The beauty of the letter was it was clear—the league office is not going to tell you how to hire coaches and the league office is not going to impose a quota system," Pash remembers. "I think people had comfort given who was on the committee, that it would be sensible, it would be respectful of the prerogatives of ownership and it would seek to identify solutions that would be consistent with how businesses do things in an intelligent way when they're trying to address issues of diversity and inclusion."

The letter encompassed the balance and credibility the owners expected from Dan Rooney.

PITTSBURGH STEELERS
3400 South Water Street
Pittsburgh, PA 15203

October 31, 2002

Paul Tagliabue
Commissioner
National Football League
280 Park Avenue
New York, New York 10017

Dear Paul:

In summary, please consider these thoughts on racial diversity in coaching and team front offices, and the potential for accelerating progress in these areas.

The Commissioner and League staff do not hire coaches or club executives. You cannot; the clubs and owners do and must.

The Commissioner and League staff have lead with a strong commitment to diversity and best practices on diversity in club hiring. With Gene Upshaw, George Young and others, you developed and implemented a number of initiatives to assist the clubs.

Individually and collectively, ownership now has to determine what now needs to be done at the club level to ensure true diversity.

The Steelers strongly recommend you proceed on this basis.

Sincerely,

Dan Rooney

The letter from Dan Rooney to Paul Tagliabue

Ray Anderson, now the athletic director for Arizona State University, had been an agent for Dungy and Green and then went to work for the Atlanta Falcons and later the NFL office. He recalls the mood among owners as a cross between panic and hopefulness.

"They knew the jig was up," said Anderson, who was a member of the working group of team executives within the diversity committee Dan Rooney chaired. "They had been flushed out into the open. I don't think there was real resistance. It was just, how do we go about it in the most efficient way?"

The rule would come to have Rooney's name, but it had the fingerprints of many others from throughout the league on it, too, especially the members of the diversity committee, which included the Falcons' Arthur Blank, the Rams' Stan Kroenke, the Broncos' Pat Bowlen and the Eagles' Jeff Lurie.

The backgrounds of Blank and Lurie were especially noteworthy. Blank made his fortune as one of the founders of Home Depot and had a long history of championing diversity in the workplace. As owner of the Philadelphia Eagles, Lurie made his first significant hire the appointment of Rhodes to be head coach in 1995. In 1999, the team drafted a black quarterback, Donovan McNabb, with the second overall pick in the NFL Draft.

At that very first meeting between Mehri and league representatives, though, there was significant resistance as the conversation turned to possible remedies. Henderson exploded at the idea proposed by Mehri that draft picks would be taken away from teams that did not abide by a diversity rule—"that will never happen," he told the group. The owners would also not accept a quota system. Mehri knew that was a non-starter from his work with the corporations with whom he had already reached settlements. Nor would owners stand for the league office telling them what to do. Dan, too, knew that the suggestion that draft picks should be surrendered was impractical and something that would not be accepted. But he did think that clear discipline would be an essential part of whatever rule was formulated—as would soon become obvious.

John Wooten was a former player and a longtime team personnel executive, and as soon as he saw Mehri's report, he told Mehri he would work with him to help promote and prepare minority coaches. He called Mehri when he heard that Dan Rooney would be in charge of the league's diversity committee. He knew well Dan's standing with other owners.

"We have just won," Wooten remembers remarking to Mehri about Dan Rooney. "This man will help us."

TWELVE

CHANGING THE CULTURE

DAN ROONEY HAD SPENT A LIFETIME STEPPING INTO CHALLENGING SITUATIONS and trying to create a sense of belonging for others. Building consensus among the team owners—while also developing a diverse hiring policy that would have credence among coaches and fans—was critical to establishing the Rooney Rule. Giving it the best chance for success, he knew, would require giving owners and others in the league the tools they needed to broaden the candidate pools.

Once the NFL's diversity committee was established, Rooney worked to ensure support for the rule it would craft and the resources needed to make the policy meaningful.

A series of meetings at Heinz Field and conference calls through November and December were an indication of Rooney's urgency to get something done. NFL owners and general managers almost never meet so often during the football season. In these meetings, my father did little talking initially, just as he had in labor negotiations and in Ireland. He rarely took a strong position unless he could build consensus around it.

Dan focused on the nuts and bolts of the hiring process. He knew that owners could not simply be handed a mandate to interview minority candidates. They needed to be given the means to find those candidates. He concentrated, Pash remembers, on doing a lot of work on things that, under any set of circumstances, would be useful, that would be consistent with the goals of diversity but were also entirely unobjectionable. For instance, he wanted to have a book of top candidates—not just minority candidates—for coaching and eventually general manager jobs which would be put together from broad input. That way, when an owner asked, "Who is out there?" there would be a tool to help him find people with whom he might otherwise be unfamiliar, to expand the universe of candidates beyond those he might have already heard of from his inner circle.

He assumed owners would accept practical tools. He thought they wanted to make good hiring decisions. But he was not as sure that owners would accept a rule that had a mandatory element to it, and he absolutely knew that could not be the solution with which they were presented.

Dan was greatly concerned about the possibility that any mandate to interview minority candidates would lead some teams to conduct sham interviews, bringing in minority candidates who never had a real chance at getting the job, just to check the box and satisfy the league's requirement. It was a fear he shared with other members of the committee. It would be humiliating for the candidates and it would reveal an owner who engaged in such behavior to be cynical and not truly committed to diversity.

Williamson played a big role in explaining to the committee members that sham interviews were a theoretical concern. While he could not assure it would never happen, he did not consider it a real roadblock. Williamson told the committee that when people sit down to conduct interviews, they do them in a serious-minded way. Whatever the risk that some owners would be less than sincere in their openness, it was worth it to get more people from diverse backgrounds in the door and into the process. Williamson said that he, in turn, would tell any coach who was invited to interview to go through with it, even if that coach thought he had almost no chance of landing the job. First, he would tell them, you never know what will happen. And second, there was something to be learned from every interview and, if nothing else, practice was good. As optimistic as Williamson's arguments were, my father's own concerns about sham interviews were never completely allayed.

That sham interviews remain an issue to this day is a reflection of one of the frailties of the rule. It relies on owners and executives to be open to new people and ideas when hiring. Given the range of backgrounds of some owners—and, in some cases, the aggressive business practices they used in their other lines of work—that is probably too much to hope for from all of them.

There was a faction in the league that was concerned that creating any kind of rule would open a Pandora's box of attendant problems. Someone would surely be offended and there was the reality that in a business, the goal is to offend as few people as possible. Perhaps, some thought, the NFL would be better off not coming up with a rule at all.

That was an idea Dan Rooney and Paul Tagliabue flatly rejected. Bill Polian, the Colts' president who had hired Dungy and was a member of the working group under the diversity committee, remembers Tagliabue telling owners that the time had passed for inch-by-inch movement, that it was time to take a firm stand and a big step.

The Madden report proposed some potential remedies that Mehri highlighted. The concept of requiring a team to interview a diverse slate of candidates was one of those. Williamson had worked with other corporations to expand opportunities within senior level management and he, too, favored the diverse slate concept.

Dan's history with creating a meritocracy with Noll for the Steelers in the 1970s dovetailed with Mehri's and Williamson's ideas and he embraced the diverse slate idea immediately. It appealed to his sense that there were multiple high-quality candidates who just needed to be given the chance to compete on a level playing field, while still not intruding on the team's right to make individual hiring decisions.

During the committee meetings, there was still considerable back and forth about what would work. My father would later tell Mehri what the dynamics of those meetings were like. Williamson would present part of Mehri's proposal and go through the good and bad of it. And members of the committee would inevitably try to shoot holes in it. "What about this? What about the token interviews?" And Williamson would reply, "OK, we have to do something. Does anyone have a better idea?"

The "diverse slate" was to cover candidates of all ethnicities—including white candidates. But the committees wanted to go a step further, to make it clear they wanted at least one minority candidate interviewed.

Dan had conversations, often one-on-one, with his fellow owners, in which they voiced their concerns. Dallas Cowboys owner Jerry Jones, a powerful voice among owners then as he is now, was resistant to the league office telling owners what to do at all, a philosophy he maintains to this day.

My father told Jones and others that the diverse slate idea would enhance their teams and the entire league because it would ensure that at least one minority coach was on every team's interview list, thus exposing owners to more quality candidates. It would, of course, also expand opportunities for minority coaches, too. Rooney told the owners it was a win-win-win if at least one minority candidate would be considered for a head coaching position. He pointed to the Steelers' success and their history of inclusive hiring as one of the primary examples of the merits of considering a broader range of candidates.

"Remember, this wasn't 50 or 100 years ago," Arthur Blank said. "People understood what was right. They were more interested in how the process would work and interested in, 'Could it be effective?' There was no point passing a rule that couldn't work. We needed to make sure that whatever they came up with was practical and you could do it."

By December, in a memo signed by each committee member and sent to all owners, the committee proposed the interview policy that came to be known as the Rooney Rule. It recommended that teams make a commitment to interview minority candidates for every head coach job and establish a databank of coordinators and assistant coaches to help teams learn about qualified candidates. The committee framed their policy proposal as affirmative outreach. The goal was to identify and hire coaches through a competitive process, not to give any group a leg up on another. Essentially the rule told owners: You just have to interview someone who doesn't look like you.

"It's not asking that much," Mehri said. "We're fighting so hard for something that is so little." That, my mother remembers, is how my father thought, too. This should not be that hard. He simply expected people to do the right thing.

Tagliabue thinks that one of the reasons my father was so good at getting consensus was that he was so often ambiguous about what he was talking about. During labor negotiations, when the league would have 30 pages of issues that represented its opinion, Dan would come back from talking to the union leaders and give Tagliabue a scrap of paper on which four vague negotiating points were scribbled. Rooney would tell Tagliabue that was the deal and Tagliabue, incredulous, would ask how that could be the deal when the league had many more points to negotiate and there was no detail about what had been agreed to. No, Dan would tell him, that's what we are negotiating right now. Then he would go back to the union leaders and do the same thing with them, slowly bringing them along, too. Then, when the other owners were apprised of negotiations and were given only the most general information, Dan would tell the other owners that he and the commissioner knew what the details were but they couldn't tell all the owners because they didn't want the details to leak to the media.

"He had a way of just slowly but surely getting people to say, 'Yeah, I can agree to that if …' " Tagliabue remembers. And then Dan would say, "If, well, don't give me too many ifs, you know. I don't want to talk about ifs today. That's tomorrow."

"Leadership is risks," Tagliabue continued. "Getting the CBA, or the Rooney Rule, nobody knew if the thing could work. People used to say, well, how do we know this can work? And Dan would say, 'I don't know if it can work, but if you've got a better alternative, tell me what it is.' "

There was a consensus about the policy proposed, but Tagliabue, Rooney and the diversity committee strongly believed there had to be unanimity to convey the league's commitment.

Al Davis of the Oakland Raiders and Mike Brown of the Cincinnati Bengals were the two owners who offered resistance. There was some arm-twisting to get them aboard.

Davis never intended to vote no, said Amy Trask, the Raiders' former chief executive officer. Davis was not opposed to the intent of the rule. He was frustrated and angered that anybody needed such a rule.

Davis had long been well ahead of most other owners on diversity. In addition to hiring the first African-American coach of the modern era in Shell, he employed Tom Flores, the first minority coach to win a Super Bowl when the Raiders won in 1981, and he made Trask the highest-ranking woman at an NFL franchise.

Because so many others considered him a pariah, Davis was not involved in negotiating the rule. He told Trask to get on one of the conference calls with the other owners on his behalf.

Trask stated the Raiders' position, that there should not need to be a rule mandating doing what is right. The Raiders, though, would not object to it, Trask told the others. "So the way we took that was, 'Al, you're already doing it and certainly you don't oppose having other people do it the Raider way, so we'll take you as in favor,' " Pash said.

Mike Brown of the Bengals was a little bit different. He, too, is a frequent contrarian. His objection was rooted in the feeling that the league office expected to face all along—that team owners have the right to hire whom they want.

Brown essentially said that while the league could send him the list of minority candidates and the book with their backgrounds, it was his franchise, his payroll, and he was going to make the decision without interference. Brown was certainly not the only owner who felt that way, but the others, including Jones, had already decided to go along with the group on a yes vote. Brown was, until almost the end, the only one who felt so strongly that the league not have a say in whom he hires that he would be the only one to vote against the new rule.

My father appealed to the Brown family history. Mike Brown's father—the famed coach Paul Brown, who had founded the Cleveland Browns and later the Cincinnati Bengals—did not get enough recognition for the work he had done for diversity in the NFL at a time when there was still real resistance from some owners to desegregating their teams.

In the earliest days of the various professional football leagues, there had been a handful of African-American players. A year before Jackie Robinson integrated Major League Baseball in 1947, Kenny Washington, a halfback and defensive back from UCLA, signed with the Rams, becoming the first African-American player in the modern NFL. The Rams had just moved to Los Angeles from Cleveland and had been told by the Los Angeles Coliseum Commission that they would have to integrate their team with at least one black player in order to lease the Coliseum.

That same year, the Cleveland Browns led by Paul Brown—who were then playing in the rival All-America Football Conference before it merged with the NFL—signed Marion Motley and Bill Willis, both of whom were black.

Wooten joined Rooney in talking about all that Paul Brown had done to promote diversity and fairness. My father explained to Mike Brown that the new rule was not an attack on him or his team. Rooney knew that neither Brown nor Davis would be able to convince other owners to join them in opposition, but having that unanimous vote was an important bit of symbolism. Dan chose to use his persuasive skills to bring them along.

The irony is that while Mike Brown might have been the last person to agree to vote for the rule, he actually did the best job of implementing it. In 2003, he hired Marvin Lewis to be the Bengals' head coach, the first African-American coach hired after the rule was put in place. Lewis transformed the Bengals in his 16 years on the job from a league laughingstock. They went to the playoffs in his third season and six more times after that.

THIRTEEN

CHAMPION

THE RULE—A HANDSHAKE AGREEMENT AMONG OWNERS—was announced publicly in late December 2002, and it should have been a moment of triumph. But within days, the rule had already been flouted by one of the league's most visible teams.

This challenge would provide Dan Rooney with a final test and the last major contribution he would make to the NFL. He would become the champion, not just the namesake, of the Rooney Rule, working for years to confront and convince owners to abide by the rule they had agreed to. That he still faced resistance to following the rule bewildered and frustrated him, but his continued involvement in promoting diversity was critical to its expansion.

Still, the rule got off to a difficult start. Jerry Jones, in need of a coach after the Cowboys finished the 2002 season 5-11 under Dave Campo, conducted just a cursory phone interview with Dennis Green before he hired Bill Parcells to coach the Cowboys. Parcells was a two-time Super Bowl winner and had been sought after for practically every opening. But Jones had simply ignored the intent of the new rule.

"I remember calling up Williamson and saying, 'What the hell, we can't even make it through one week?' " Mehri said.

My father was upset—he moved through life simply expecting people to live up to their word. If an owner said he supported the new rule, he expected him to abide by it. But he was also a realist. He knew it was impossible to criticize the hiring of a coach the stature of Parcells. And because the Cowboys could claim to have technically followed the letter of the rule with Dennis Green's phone interview, Dan did not think this was a strong enough case to impose discipline for the first time.

Moreover, Dan worried that penalizing the Cowboys could set off a fight with Jones, who would be a formidable adversary capable of drawing other owners to his side. That would doom the fragile consensus that had just been formed. And Dan Rooney knew there was likely to be another—clearer—violation of the rule that would demand discipline.

Alas, he was correct. The league did not discipline Jones. But shortly after, Matt Millen, then the president of the Detroit Lions, failed to interview even one minority candidate before he hired Steve Mariucci as the team's next head coach. Millen said he had tried to interview several minority candidates, but they had turned the Lions down, because they figured Mariucci was already a lock to be hired.

My father called Lions owner William Clay Ford. He was not looking for a confrontation, but rather an explanation of Ford's thinking, while also explaining to Ford his point of view. Dan Rooney issued a statement saying the Lions had fallen short of what the committee recommended, but internally there was no real need for him to push for discipline. It was a clear-cut case and Tagliabue saw it that way, too. That summer, Tagliabue fined Millen $200,000.

A more subtle, but no less important, development for the rule took place around the same time, at a meeting of coaches, scouts and front office personnel who were gathered in Indianapolis for the annual Scouting Combine of college players. There, the Fritz Pollard Alliance, an affinity group of NFL coaches, scouts and front office personnel, many of them black, was formed. The purpose of the Alliance was to work with the league office and teams to advocate for minority candidates for jobs in leadership positions. They would debrief owners and candidates about how interviews went and they would ask owners for feedback on how candidates could improve in interviews. They produced a 10-

page guide for potential candidates on how to prepare for interviews—questions they might face, who might be in the room. Dan thought the tools the Alliance established would enhance the interview process and he took great interest in assisting them. He did not just work on the Rooney Rule at a strategic level. He worked at the technical level, to support the Alliance's efforts to improve the interview process.

The Alliance was the NFL equivalent of a test prep class, giving candidates the information they need to ace the most critical exams of their careers. And it also acts as a watchdog group, alerting the league and media about teams that do not comply with the rule, a job that is still among its most important duties.

At that meeting in Indianapolis, John Wooten was made the chairman of the Alliance. Wooten and Dan worked together for more than a decade—they spoke nearly every day—as the most significant champions of the NFL's push for greater diversity in hiring coaches.

As a young boy, Wooten attended segregated schools in Carlsbad, New Mexico, before transferring to the newly integrated Carlsbad High School. His heroes were Joe Louis and Jackie Robinson. He was the first person in his family to go to college, and while at the University of Colorado, he became the second African-American varsity football player in the school's history.

Wooten played for Paul Brown as a Browns offensive lineman. After Wooten retired, he became the director of professional scouting for the Dallas Cowboys and later worked for the Eagles and the Ravens. Still, because he had never held a top coaching or general manager job, Wooten was relatively unknown among NFL brass. He and Dan, though, worked together for years after the Rooney Rule went into place—and until my father's death—forming the underpinnings and infrastructure that continue to give the policy a chance at success.

Theirs was a unique partnership, driven by my father's interest in the issue above and beyond his own personal interest in the NFL. He was willing to work with an outside group like the Alliance that may have criticized the NFL for its hiring practices because he thought such a partnership would pay greater dividends. It was the same tactic he had also employed as he built a partnership and grew close with Gene Upshaw, who headed the players' union, during labor negotiations.

Dan would sometimes visit Mehri at his Washington, D.C., office and he confided in Mehri and Wooten his frustrations with his fellow owners and with their decision-making. Dan told Mehri he couldn't believe some owners would overreact during coaching searches, trying to appease media and fans rather than conducting a thorough process for their most critical hire. And he was flummoxed by an owner who did not take their time with their searches.

"I don't understand—this is the most important decision you make as an owner," Mehri recalled my father saying at one visit. "I don't understand why guys rush into it."

It was Wooten who first suggested to Rooney that the Rooney Rule be expanded to general manager openings—a change made in 2009—and the Alliance was also a proponent of having more diversity among game officials.

Wooten and Dan developed an essential partnership. Dan dedicated time and his reputation to pushing for more minority coaches and he used his access to decision-makers to put the issue on the front burner. Wooten, though, became the full-time leader of the effort.

Wooten and Rooney talked regularly about the "ready list," a list that the Alliance developed each year of head coaching and general manager candidates who they felt were prepared to take on bigger jobs. The Alliance monitored coaches and executives during the year and kept in constant touch with Dan Rooney and other league officials about who they were thinking of putting on the list. Before the "ready list" was finalized for the league around December, Rooney would take the list and do his own research. He relied on Steelers coaches Bill Cowher and Mike Tomlin and Kevin Colbert, then the Steelers' director of player personnel, for information on a list that could number up to 40 candidates each year. Colbert would rate candidates and give Rooney details about what he knew about each coach. Then Dan would work with Wooten to review which candidates he thought were ready for head jobs and what concerns he had about other candidates.

The rule was personal to Dan Rooney. He often made calls to other owners at Wooten's behest, imploring them to allow lower-level scouts or position coaches to make vertical moves at other teams, even though they were under contract.

Those jobs were not covered by the Rooney Rule, but giving those coaches and scouts opportunities to enhance their resumes and gain broader experience helped to better prepare them for future jobs, and it increased the number of minority assistant coaches by 40 percent. Every year, Wooten called Dan when a team would not let someone leave for another job and Rooney would intercede.

Wooten and my father also talked regularly about the problem of sham interviews, with my father telling Wooten repeatedly that if some owners are not looking at all of the top-quality candidates, they are simply hurting themselves and their teams.

"I could never have imagined how deeply Rooney would commit to his partnership with John Wooten," Mehri said.

After the New York Jets fired Rex Ryan at the end of the 2014 season, they wanted to interview their assistant head coach, Anthony Lynn, for the job. Lynn had never interviewed for a head job before and he didn't want to go through this interview either—he suspected that the Jets wanted to interview him just to fulfill the Rooney Rule's requirement to interview a minority candidate, potentially the kind of sham interview Dan feared.

Wooten encouraged Lynn to go through with the interview. The people assisting the Jets' search—former general managers Charley Casserly and Ron Wolf, among others—had many connections around the league and, Wooten told him, it would be beneficial for Lynn to see what the interviews are like and what owners are looking for. Lynn went to the interview, deciding that he would be someone's "Rooney Rule" interview only one time and never again. He told the Jets up front that he was going to ask as many questions as they would ask him, so he could learn about the process. The interview lasted five hours. Lynn didn't get the job—Todd Bowles, another African-American coach, did—but the next year, when Lynn was again working for Ryan in Buffalo, his name began circulating as a head coaching candidate. And after the 2016 season—two years after that first interview with the Jets—the Los Angeles Chargers made Lynn their new head coach.

"They spread my name a little bit," Lynn said. "I think a little exposure—something good did come of it."

Dan Rooney and John Wooten were the champions the cause needed. Criticism of the outcomes, particularly recently, are warranted and necessary if the rule is to continue to be relevant. But it's impossible to imagine the system working for coaches like Lynn years after the rule was put in place without the diligence and completeness of the efforts Wooten and Rooney made together.

The fulfillment of my father's commitment to diversity—first on display when he hired Bill Nunn—was embodied by Mike Tomlin.

Tomlin had been on the Fritz Pollard Alliance's radar already and Wooten was among those who encouraged Dan Rooney to take a look at the young defensive coordinator when he needed a successor to Cowher. One of the most meaningful moments of that process, Tomlin says now, came at the very beginning, before he even had an interview. Dungy, for whom Tomlin had worked in Tampa, and Wooten both called him to let him know of the Steelers' interest. And they each told Tomlin that the Rooney Rule requirement had already been met.

To Tomlin, that was the essence of the rule. Dan Rooney had deliberately slowed down the process so he could talk to a range of people, including those he did not know. During the interview, Rooney asked Tomlin a series of questions that touched on all aspects of the business. "What's your belief regarding blah blah blah, what is your belief regarding …?" Tomlin remembers. My father was trying to get an assessment of Tomlin's core values.

Tomlin and my father grew close after he got the job in 2007. In the early days, Rooney tried to get Tomlin to call him "Dan," something Tomlin would not do. Each morning, Tomlin had a team meeting at 9 a.m. and when it would end, he would walk down to Rooney's office with its windows overlooking the practice fields and the two would sit and talk, often about their children and their lives.

If Dan Rooney hadn't liked what he heard when he asked Tomlin about his core values, he would not have hired him, no matter his skin color. But Tomlin allowed my father to do something that was the culmination of the biggest passion of his life. The results on the field support my father's belief he was the best man for the job. In his second year with the Steelers, Tomlin became the youngest head coach, and the second African-American head coach, to win a Super Bowl. Two years later, the Steelers were in the Super Bowl again.

The Steelers have been to the playoffs in eight of Tomlin's 12 seasons and his .654 winning percentage through 2018 ranks him 15th all-time.

The significance of his hire, five years after the creation of the Rooney Rule, went far beyond the wins column. It was lost on no one, least of all Tomlin himself.

"I think that that was probably the most challenging aspect of the opportunity for me early on," Tomlin said. "I knew what my hiring meant to him. I knew what it short term meant, long term meant, what my hiring meant, and I didn't want to let him down. I know that he didn't view it in that way, but boy I did. It went beyond doing the job for me, and always will, because I understand it. I've always understood it, and knew that how we performed was critical to the shaping of the legacy of his in some way. That legacy is so devoted. It's really been a guiding force for me, in terms of having the desire to perform.

"I know he didn't want me to feel that way, but I felt that way nonetheless. How could you not?"

Eric Holder, who served as outside counsel to the league prior to becoming attorney general of the United States, paid what might be the most significant compliments to my father's work when he compared my father to the general manager of the Brooklyn Dodgers who broke baseball's color barrier by signing Jackie Robinson.

Holder said, "Mr. Rooney's contributions, in his day, can be compared to those of Branch Rickey."

Tony Dungy and Chuck Noll | Courtesy of Pittsburgh Steelers

Dan Rooney and Mike Tomlin | Courtesy of Pittsburgh Steelers

Craig Richardson, Jeremi Duru, Suritia Taylor, John Wooten, Cyrus Mehri, Harry Carson
Wallace Faggett/Fritz Pollard Alliance

Mike Tomlin, Kevin Colbert, Dan Rooney | Courtesy of Pittsburgh Steelers

Cyrus Mehri, Jim Brown, Harry Carson | Wallace Faggett/Fritz Pollard Alliance

Jeremi Duru and John Wooten | Wallace Faggett/Fritz Pollard Alliance

Tony Dungy and Mike Wagner | Courtesy of Pittsburgh Steelers

Roger Goodell, Dan Rooney, John Wooten | Wallace Faggett/Fritz Pollard Alliance

CONCLUSION

This book tells the story of my father's life. It is my hope that his story provides some insight and, more so, some inspiration. I certainly hope readers have enjoyed it. I also believe my father would have felt a review of his life in such a public fashion would be of value if it were to serve some benefit going forward. In order to accomplish that I have taken some time and spoken with some top business and hiring experts to understand the limits, effectiveness and best potential pathways forward, particularly with the Rooney Rule, for the work that was my father's life.

As the first African-American head coach hired after the Rooney Rule's enactment, Marvin Lewis could not avoid the rule's shadow. He turned around a dreadful Bengals team that had gone 2-14 the year before, guided them to an 8-8 record, and barely missed the playoffs. In 16 seasons, Lewis became the winningest head coach in Bengals history. He was named the Coach of the Year following the 2009 season.

Lewis' hire in 2003 returned the number of NFL head coaches of color to the previous all-time high of three. The following year, there were five. By 2007, there were six. The number of head coaches of color fluctuated over the course of the next few years, but in 2011, it reached eight, quadrupling in the eight years since the Rooney Rule had taken effect. Teams were following the rule, and it was changing the league. The league had expanded the rule to apply also to searches for general managers. And the numbers have increased there as well. By the start of the 2017 season, a once nearly unthinkable 14 NFL teams employed a head coach or general manager of color, and since the Rooney Rule's enactment, clubs had hired 14 different head coaches of color and 12 different general managers of color. Notably, many of the head coaches and general managers hired under the rule have taken their clubs to the sport's pinnacle. Since 2007, 10 clubs featuring a head coach or general manager of color have reached the Super Bowl.

The spirit of the rule has been crucial as well. The Rooney Rule does not apply to assistant coach positions. However, since the rule was implemented, the percentage of minority assistant coaches in the league has increased by 40 percent. The Rooney Rule also does not formally apply to selection of game day officials. Still, the values that the rule has helped drive into the NFL's culture—the importance of equal opportunity and casting a wide net—adhere in that context. Consequently, in the league's Officiating Development Program, which contains 35 collegiate officials, 18 (51.4 percent) are minority and three are female.

Still, there is reason for concern about the NFL's future on diversity. A 2019 ESPN study explored all 108 off-season head coach hires that NFL teams had made between the rule's inception in 2003 and the end of the 2018 season. Fifteen years later, despite the Rooney Rule's implementation and all of the progress the league had experienced, ESPN's study revealed that "minority coaches aren't given tenures as long as their white counterparts, although they win more frequently."

While sobering, such a realization should not have been surprising. Minority head coaching aspirants had been discriminated against and overlooked in the NFL for three-quarters of a century before the rule's enactment. A tilted playing field is not easily leveled. Nevertheless, with the rule in place, progress was slow, but it seemed steady.

The first season after my father died revealed a new potential weakness in the rule that few had thought about: Might the rule's success depend inordinately on the leadership, advocacy and moral authority of a few people?

My mother, Patricia Rooney, said, "Maybe they thought when he left, the rule left."

My father passed away on April 13, 2017. That same year, John Wooten began to share quietly with close friends and colleagues that he intended to retire as chairman of the Fritz Pollard Alliance shortly after the 2018 Super Bowl.

During the 2017 hiring cycle, teams at best had failed to abide by the spirit of the Rooney Rule. At least one displeased club owner called the league office, insisting that teams would not have handled their searches the way that they did, and that the league would not have countenanced it, had my father been alive. My father did not hold unlimited sway over his fellow owners or the commissioner and his deputies, but he was a consistent voice in their ears. When he passed away, that voice was gone, and the rule did not operate as it should have. The rule must be deeply woven into an organization's culture, and a consistent commitment from internal leadership is critical, even more important than external pressure.

The 2017 hiring season taught that the rule alone is not enough. Accountability is crucial. The league's diversity committee, with help from the Fritz Pollard Alliance, pushed for greater accountability to strengthen the rule. Beginning in December 2018, teams are required to interview either an external candidate or a candidate on the list of prospective minority head coaches that the NFL and the Fritz Pollard Alliance put together each year. In addition, an owner must now be involved in all interviews, not just some of them. The revised rule also requires clubs to maintain and, upon the commissioner's request, produce all records regarding hiring processes to which the Rooney Rule applies.

The one addition that seems an obvious enhancement, which the league did not implement, was a requirement that each club interview at least two candidates of color before making a hire. In 2016, the Harvard Business Review published an article highlighting three statistical studies on the Rooney Rule conducted by a team of researchers at the University of Colorado. Those studies revealed that when only one minority or woman was in a final pool of candidates for a position, the chances of the woman or minority getting the position were slim. However, "[w]hen there were two minorities or women in the pool of finalists, the status quo changed, resulting in a woman or minority becoming the favored candidate." Specifically, they found that having two women in the final interview pool made the odds of hiring a woman 79.14 times greater and that two people of color in the final interview pool made the odds of hiring a minority 193.72 times greater.

Two years later, a separate Harvard Business Review article revealed that having "two in the pool" was important in the NFL as well. That article, which focused specifically on NFL hiring between 2013 and 2017, revealed that of the 35 head coaches hired over the course of those five years, 29 were white and six were of color. The authors found that in 22 of those 35 instances, only one coach of color was interviewed, and on only one of those 22 occasions when one coach of color was interviewed—less than 5 percent of the time—was a coach of color hired. Given that on average roughly five coaching candidates are interviewed for each position, chance alone would suggest a coach of color should be hired 20 percent of the time. By contrast, of the 12 instances in which two or more coaches of color were interviewed, a coach of color was hired four times (33 percent of the time).

In 2018, a second troubling factor arose. For years, NFL rules changes had evolved to protect quarterbacks and favor offenses. Because of the emphasis on offense, many team owners had come to prefer offensive coaches to become their head coaches.

During the 2018 season, 10 of the league's 32 defensive coordinators were of color, while only two of the league's 32 offensive coordinators were of color. This was no coincidence. Offensive coordinators and quarterbacks coaches— the most desired head coaching candidates—were often former quarterbacks themselves. And for generations, vile stereotypes about the intelligence and leadership capabilities of black athletes had prevented teams from allowing African-Americans to play quarterback at any level.

My father thought those stereotypes were ludicrous. He took the same approach to the sport's marquee position as his coach. Noll's naming of Joe Gilliam as the first black quarterback to start a season in 1974 was proof.

The hiring cycle that followed the 2018 season revealed this challenge to coaching diversity to be a reality. Only one of the eight hired head coaches—Brian Flores, the defensive play caller for the New England Patriots who was hired by the Miami Dolphins—is a person of color. Just four head coaches of color started the 2019 season—a 50 percent drop from the previous year.

That result is less than stellar. However, these challenges to implementation should not overshadow the fundamental strength of the rule. Its driving forces are a concerted effort to identify diverse talent, thus creating new opportunities that align with the fundamental fairness we all expect in the workplace. They leave merit as the final criteria in hiring. People making hiring decisions need to feel they are choosing the best candidate once they have conducted a thorough process. Every minority coach we spoke with expressed that he clearly wanted to earn his position, not to have something given to him. This essential balance is the basis of the Rooney Rule and why people beyond football have become so interested in its application for their use.

My father did live to see the beginning of the rule's traction in America's public and private sectors. No iteration of the Rooney Rule has the potential for more meaningful and expansive impact than that rolled out in the U.S. Congress in 2017. In February of that year, the Senate Democrats adopted a version of the Rooney Rule, unanimously agreeing that before hiring for any staff position, they will interview a diverse slate of candidates. At the time, only one senator had an African-American chief of staff—Senator Tim Scott, a Republican from South Carolina, who is African-American. With the Rooney Rule in place, aspiring politicians and bureaucrats from populations largely frozen out of Washington's power circles have increased access to the opportunity that an interview provides. And, just as important, some of Washington's most influential power brokers and policymakers—senators, almost all of whom are white—gain exposure to candidates, and potentially employees, who represent the diversity of our nation.

This is, of course, no less true of the House of Representatives, and four months after Senator Chuck Schumer led Senate Democrats to adopt the Rooney Rule for staff hiring, Speaker Nancy Pelosi did the same in the House. As the Rooney Rule is not partisan and takes into account both opportunity as well as merit in hiring decisions (concepts both the left and the right agree upon), it would be great if Republicans followed the lead of their colleague, Tim Scott, and instituted a Congress-wide Rooney Rule.

The tech industry was at the forefront of the Rooney Rule's private sector expansion, and although my father did not have great familiarity with tech, he was thrilled with its embrace of the rule.

As the senior vice president of people operations for Google, Laszlo Bock was responsible for creating one of the most recognized and, by many measures, best corporate cultures ever to be developed.

As the company continued to grow, several challenges emerged. One was how to create greater diversity, particularly with an African-American workforce. Similar to many technical skills, software coding was not an area in which large groups of African-Americans had received training. As a result, there was a large deficit in hiring of African-Americans at the search engine giant.

Bock felt an obligation to attend to this problem. He would regularly meet with peers, the other members of the CEO's staff, to talk about inclusion. Over a decade, Bock led Google executives in reviewing progress in hiring, retention, career progression, promotion rates and how underrepresented Google employees felt in their workplace. Beginning in 2006, Google made steady, though slow, progress.

Because of Bock's role, he was well-versed in the Rooney Rule process. However, in learning about Dan Rooney and John Wooten's work as advocates who were constantly pushing for specific opportunities and consideration of candidates in specific situations, especially at the assistant coach level (which again, is not covered by the Rooney Rule), Bock claimed, "that is exactly what needs to happen if these initiatives will ever achieve significant success. … People at the leadership level as well as those at the execution level have to be committed, not only to the policies but to the actions that make them real, and it appears Dan Rooney did both."

"When it comes to inclusion, sustained effort matters. In fact, it's necessary. And in the absence of someone pushing hard—for years!—companies and people revert to their old, biased ways," he continued.

Bock left Google to create a new organization, Humu, a Silicon Valley start-up. It uses artificial intelligence to build on some concepts of the people-analytics programs pioneered by the internet giant, which has included things like the traits that define great managers, how to identify the capabilities of effective teams and how biases and diversity are or are not being served by an organization.

Elements of my father's approach are similar to the AI reminders Bock is bringing to the modern workplace.

On August 4, 2015, President Obama hosted the White House's first ever "Demo Day," designed to showcase innovations from around the country, with an emphasis on highlighting the contributions of women and people of color. Much like tech sector Demo Days, talented entrepreneurs detailed their ideas and inventions, but these entrepreneurs were not pitching potential funders. Rather, the White House was in a sense pitching the entrepreneurs themselves and the concept that talent comes in all colors and genders. While whites and Asian-Americans are generally well represented in tech, African-Americans and Latinos are sorely underrepresented. And among management, Asian-American women are similarly scarce. During the event, President Obama spoke passionately about the value of opportunity and the importance of diversity to success. He specifically called on companies throughout the tech industry to pursue increased workplace diversity, and they responded. A few had already been building strategies to diversify, some of which involved forms of the Rooney Rule, but Obama's call catalyzed more movement. Giants of the industry, such as Amazon, Intel and Xerox, announced in the wake of Demo Day that they would implement the Rooney Rule.

Less than a year after Demo Day, Silicon Valley received another equal opportunity jolt when concerned tech industry professionals founded Project Include. Project Include is a nonprofit organization whose mission is to "give everyone a fair chance to succeed in tech," and its recommendation that the Rooney Rule be applied in hiring for all positions throughout Silicon Valley continued the momentum that Obama's speech sparked. Companies throughout the tech sector, large and small, employ some form of the rule. A non-exhaustive list of such companies includes Amazon, Facebook, HubSpot, Intel, LinkedIn, Lyft, Microsoft, Pinterest, Slack, Uber and Xerox.

One of the Rooney Rule's great advantages is that every organization utilizing it can do so in its own particular way. This is borne out in the tech sector. For instance, Intel requires an interview slate of "two women and/or two people of color" whereas Xerox more generally demands a "diverse slate of candidates." And whereas Lyft has a policy that applies to all hires at the director level, Amazon applies the rule at the very top, requiring that at least one woman or minority is interviewed for each opening on the board of directors.

While the pursuit of fairness and equity may have partially motivated the decision-makers at these companies, business considerations no doubt played a part as well. Much like my father's approach with the Steelers, these companies recognize that they will be more successful, and will gain a competitive advantage, if they diversify. Indeed, in the United States, there is a linear relationship between racial and ethnic diversity and better financial performance: For every 10 percent increase in diversity on the senior executive team, earnings rise 0.8

percent. Because the technology industry is one of the most influential business sectors in the United States, the Rooney Rule's presence in this industry bodes well for its continued proliferation in the private sector.

Law firms represent another realm of the private sector that has stepped forward to embrace the Rooney Rule. Under the Mansfield Rule—named after the first licensed female lawyer in the nation—dozens of major law firms have together agreed that they will "consider two or more candidates who are women or attorneys of color" when "hiring for leadership and governance roles, promotions to equity partner, and hiring lateral attorneys." Over 50 corporate legal departments across the country have followed suit. And Wall Street may be following suit as well. In March 2019, Goldman Sachs announced that it would implement the Rooney Rule concept in an effort to diversify its workforce. Under the initiative, all of the bank's managers are required to interview at least two diverse candidates for every open position. With Goldman Sachs—one of the world's largest and most respected investment banks—leading, other Wall Street firms could well follow.

The Rooney Rule will forever be a part of my father's legacy, and he would be proud of that. That legacy fundamentally changed the way that we pursue equal opportunity.

However, on a personal note, I know the moment that meant so much to my father happened on May 23, 2011, when President Obama and First Lady Michelle Obama visited Ireland. The last stop of the trip was a respite at the ambassador's residence, the home my father and mother were stewards of on behalf of the United States of America. He cherished the private time to connect with the president and first lady. A couple of hours earlier, Ambassador Rooney got to stand on a stage in front of a crowd of 100,000 and introduce the Taoiseach, or prime minister, of Ireland and the first African-American president of the United States.

This moment and opportunity represented so much of my father's life: his commitment to fairness and equity in the context of the American civil rights struggle and his devotion to his ancestral homeland, where he had spent so much time during the Troubles, trying to find paths forward for all. Professionally, I know the accomplishments of the Steelers' Super Bowl championships and the team's role as Pittsburgh's representative in the National Football League meant the most to him. But to have the chance to stand on the world stage and embrace the dignity, unity and hope of such a moment was, I imagine, like no other for him.

The moment encapsulated the story of my father's life. He always considered long-range goals when trying to solve a problem. He cajoled, prodded and coaxed friends and foes alike to find their "better angels" to try and get them to do the right thing. And he applied unwavering diligence and rigor in pursuit of balance and equity. This truly was his best example of a different way to win.

ACKNOWLEDGMENTS

Pete Abitante
Greg Aiello
Doug Allen
John Allison
Joe Bailey
Paxton Baker
Alec Balenciaga
Jack Barbour
Judy Battista
Stephanie Beck
Jill Berardi
Reagan Berube
Rocky Bleier
Mel Blount
Laszlo Bock
Onnie Bose
Derrick Brooks
Tim Carey
Jay Carney
Justin Chen
Kevin Colbert
David Cooper
Chuck Daly
Tony Dungy
Jeremi Duru
Herm Edwards
Patricia Rooney Gerrero
Monica Gibbons
Father Mark Glasgow
Loretta Brennan
  Glucksman
Terry Golway
Roger Goodell
Joe Gordon
Joe Greene
Randy Grossman

David Gurwin
Suzie Guzzo
John Hennessey-Niland
Eric Holder
Patricia Hume
Ryan Huzjak
Kayla Kelley
Katie Keogh
Bob Labriola
Jim Lamb
Burt Lauten
Reggie Love
Rory MacIntyre
Seamus Mallon
Capricia Penavic
  Marshall
Missi Matthews
Martin McAleese
Jackie McDonald
Kieran McLoughlin
Bill McNally
Cyrus Mehri
Kelsey Morris
Chris Noll
Marianne Noll
Tony O'Reilly
Jeff Pash
Joe Paulsen
Julie Perlish
Jason Pischke
Bill Polian
Carmen Policy
Oscar Ramirez
Jim Rohr
Duffy Rooney
Jimmy Rooney

John Rooney
Matt Rooney
Patricia Rooney
Sarah Rooney
Stephanie Rooney
Art Rooney II
Art Rooney Jr.
Dan Rooney Jr.
Karl Roser
Alvaro Saralegui
Hans Schroeder
Jon Schwartz
Gerard Schaefer
Brittany Shaffer
Donnie Shell
Ted Smyth
John Stallworth
Dean Stamoulis
Jake Sullivan
Zia Syed
Chan Tagliabue
Drew Tagliabue
Paul Tagliabue
Paul Thornell
Brian Tirpak
Mike Tomlin
Stephanie Valencia
Richard Verma
Mike Wagner
Laura Wendelin
Lynell Wilson
John Wodarek
John Wooten

SOURCES

Except where noted below, the sources for quotations and anecdotes are from interviews the author conducted from 2016 to 2018.

CHAPTER 1: Dan Rooney, *My 75 Years With The Pittsburgh Steelers and the NFL* (New York: DeCapo Press, 2007), 50; Rob Ruck, Maggie Jones Patterson, Michael P. Weber, *Rooney: A Sporting Life* (Lincoln, Nebraska: University of Nebraska Press, 2010), p. 353; Rooney, 122, 124.

CHAPTER 2: "The Mayor Surrenders Atlanta," by Jim Minter, *Sports Illustrated*, July 12, 1965; Mike Oriard, *Brand NFL: Making and Selling America's Favorite Sport* (Chapel Hill, North Carolina: University of North Carolina Press, 2007), p. 12; "In a Bid to Pick Up the Pace, The NFL Will Kill Off Everyone's Least-Favorite Ad Break," by Anthony Crupi, *AdAge*, March 22, 2017; $5.66 billion: "A Look at the Seminal Broadcasting Moves That Define the NFL." by Joe Reedy, Associated Press, Aug. 24, 2019.

CHAPTER 3: Rooney, 103; "Solidarity With Solidity," by Joe Marshall, *Sports Illustrated,* July 15, 1974; "That '70s Strike," by Emily Kaplan, *Sports Illustrated*, July 31, 2014; *The New York Times*, Oct. 4, 1992; Rooney, 179; John Mackey et al. v. National Football League, et al. Volume V testimony, 1833; Rooney, 224, 256; Michael MacCambridge, *America's Game: The Epic Story of How Pro Football Captured a Nation* (New York: Anchor Books, 2005), 384; *Newsday*, Sept. 25, 1987; David George Surdam, *Run to Glory and Profits: The Economic Rise of the NFL During the 1950s* (Lincoln, Nebraska: University of Nebraska Press, 2013), p. 330; $15 billion: "NFL Is Bullish on Its $25 Billion Revenue Goal Ahead of Super Bowl," by Scott Soshnick and Eben Novy-Williams, *Bloomberg*, Jan. 28, 2019.

CHAPTER 4: *The New York Times*, Feb. 5, 2006; *Los Angeles Times*, Jan. 21, 2011; *AdAge*, March 22, 2017.

CHAPTER 5: *Pittsburgh Post-Gazette*, June 14, 2014; Michael MacCambridge, *Chuck Noll: His Life's Work* (Pittsburgh: University of Pittsburgh Press, 2016), 12; Rooney, 159, 160.

CHAPTER 7: *The New York Times*, March 20, 1977, April 23, 1977, April 16, 1977, June 16, 1977; Maurice Fitzpatrick, *John Hume in America: From Derry to DC* (Newbridge, Ireland: Irish Academic Press, 2017), 59; *The New York Times*, April 22, 1981; *The New York Times*, Oct. 13, 1984; "Remarks at a St. Patrick's Day Reception," *The U.S. National Archives and Records Administration: Ronald Reagan Presidential Library & Museum*, March 17, 1987.

CHAPTER 8: *Pittsburgh Post-Gazette*, Sept. 11, 2005; *The Washington Post*, Dec. 9, 1984; Irish Republican Army (IRA) Ceasefire Statement, Aug. 31, 1994.

CHAPTER 9: The White House, President Barack Obama, Statement and Release, March 17, 2009; Daniel Rooney, Ambassador-Designate to Ireland. Statement Before the Senate Committee on Foreign Relations, June 24, 2009; *The Guardian*, May 23, 2011; U.S. Embassy video, Dec. 14, 2012. https://www.youtube.com/watch?v=pKWFckQ4m1o

CHAPTER 10: *The New York Times*, Jan. 4, 1998, Oct. 4, 1989.

CONCLUSION: "If There's Only One Woman in Your Candidate Pool, There's Statistically No Chance She'll Be Hired," by S.K. Johnson, D.R. Hekman and E.T. Chan, *Harvard Business Review*, April 26, 2016; "What Amazon's Board Was Getting Wrong About Diversity and Hiring," by Stefanie K. Johnson, *Harvard Business Review*, May 14, 2018; *The Washington Post*, Jan. 6, 2017; "These Big Law Firms Are Officially Diversity Certified," by Kathryn Rubino, *Above the Law*, Aug. 21, 2018; "Diversity Matters," by Vivian Hunt, Dennis Layton and Sara Prince, *McKinsey*, Feb. 2015.

PHOTO CREDIT KEY

PAGES 159-160

MINORITY HIRES

BEFORE
&
AFTER

THE ROONEY RULE

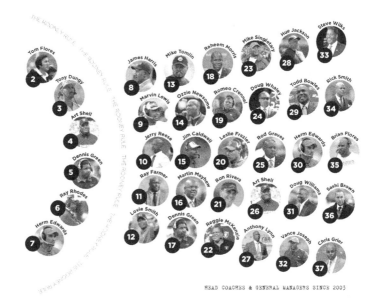

HEAD COACHES & GENERAL MANAGERS SINCE 2003

1. Fritz Pollard | Pro Football Hall of Fame/Associated Press
2. Tom Flores | Uncredited/Associated Press
3. Tony Dungy | Chris O'Meara/Associated Press
4. Art Shell | Paul Spinelli/Associated Press
5. Dennis Green | Rick Hossman/Associated Press
6. Ray Rhodes | Mark Lennihan/Associated Press
7. Herm Edwards | Charlie Riedel/Associated Press
8. James Harris | Paul Sancya/Associated Press
9. Marvin Lewis | Michael McGinnis /Associated Press
10. Jerry Reese | Bill Kostroun/Associated Press
11. Ray Farmer | Ron Schwane/Associated Press
12. Lovie Smith | David Duprey/Associated Press
13. Mike Tomlin | Gene J. Puskar/Associated Press
14. Ozzie Newsome | Greg Trott/Associated Press
15. Jim Caldwell | Paul Sancya/Associated Press
16. Martin Mayhew | Paul Sancya/Associated Press
17. Dennis Green | Rick Hossman/Associated Press
18. Raheem Morris | Chris O'Meara/Associated Press
19. Romeo Crennel | Mark Duncan/Associated Press
20. Leslie Frazier | Andy King/Associated Press
21. Ron Rivera | Chuck Burton/Associated Press
22. Reggie McKenzie | Jeff Chiu/Associated Press
23. Mike Singletary | Paul Sakuma/Associated Press
24. Doug Whaley | Bill Wippert/Associated Press
25. Rod Graves | Kevin Terrell/Associated Press
26. Art Shell | Paul Spinelli/Associated Press
27. Anthony Lynn | Kelvin Kuo/Associated Press
28. Hue Jackson | Eric Risberg/Associated Press
29. Todd Bowles | Julio Cortez/Associated Press
30. Herm Edwards | Charlie Riedel/Associated Press
31. Doug Williams | Michael Ainsworth/Associated Press
32. Vance Joseph | Eric Risberg/Associated Press
33. Steve Wilks | Matt York/Associated Press
34. Rick Smith | Stephen Brashear/Associated Press
35. Brian Flores | Wilfredo Lee/Associated Press
36. Sashi Brown | Ron Schwane/Associated Press
37. Chris Grier | Wilfredo Lee/Associated Press

Made in the USA
Coppell, TX
30 January 2020